Seeds that Change the World

Praise for *Seeds that Change the World*

"Both a compelling spiritual biography and a meaningful comment on the role of religion in contemporary society, this book answers questions yet helpfully provokes us to re-assess the now-accepted idea of faith without community."

—*James Golden, British historian*

"Debbie Humphries offers us a twenty-first century realization of the Quaker journal in its classic form. It combines personal journey and introspective insight with sustained engagement with the collective processes of Quaker faith and practice, while grappling with some of the largest social problems of our time. Not only Friends but a variety of readers will find their own journeys and challenges evoked by the chapters of this book."

— *Doug Gwyn, author of* A Sustainable Life: Quaker Faith and Practice in the Renewal of Creation

"What if you trusted the Holy presence is only revealed in respectful and honest community? What if you knew embraced insecurity reaps freedom and growth is only possible outside your comfort zone? Through these pages you are invited to walk with prophetic Debbie Humphries on the wild side of engaged and hopeful revelation, working on solutions for our deepest problems. Follow her process with your heart; you will be changed forever."

— *Cruger Johnson Phillips, LPC, Spiritual Director*

"Debbie Humphries uses her own life experience, as well as learnings from Friends past and present, to show readers (both those new to Quaker faith and practice, as well as those seasoned in the life of Quaker discipleship) that Listening for the Still, Small Voice is only the first step in a life journey of living and bearing witness to God's Love."

— *Deborah Fisch, retreat leader and former Associate Secretary of Traveling Ministries of Friends General Conference*

"In a variety of personal and inspiring essays Debbie Humphries offers seeds of hope in practices of the Quaker tradition that could transform our world."

— *Eleanor Godway, emeritus professor of philosophy, Central Connecticut State University*

Seeds that Change the World

Essays on Quakerism, Spirituality, Faith and Culture

by Debbie L. Humphries
foreword by Diane Randall

FGC

QuakerPress of FGC
Philadelphia, PA

QuakerPress of Friends General Conference
1216 Arch Street, 2B, Philadelphia, PA 19107

Printed in the United States of America

Design and layout by David Botwinik

ISBN 978-0-9993823-0-1 (paperback)
        978-0-9993823-1-8 (digital)

Library of Congress Cataloging-in-Publication Data
Humphries, Debbie, 1964–
      Seeds Which Change the World: Essays on Quakerism, Spirituality, Faith, and Culture / Debbie Humphries
      First [edition].
         pages cm
      Includes bibliographical references.
      ISBN 978-0-9993823-0-1 (paperback) (binding: soft back) 1. Society of Friends. 2. Spirituality.

All scripture quotations are taken from the New English translation of the Bible unless noted otherwise.

To order more copies of this publication or other Quaker titles call 1-800-966-4556 or see the online catalog at www.quakerbooks.org

Contents

CONTENTS

Foreword

THAT THE WORLD NEEDS QUAKERISM is a notion that I enthusiastically endorse. In this book, Debbie Humphries takes us on her personal journey as a Friend — sharing the numinous presence and the daily disciplines of our practice as Quakers. Debbie brings us into her times of reflection, her understanding, and her passion of ministry. The Quaker practices she describes of seeking, of living the questions, of embracing the wholeness in the world — these are ways of being that our world very much needs.

Becoming a Quaker opened up a new life for me, eventually leading me to the Friends Committee on National Legislation (FCNL) and a role as a public Friend. But long before I arrived at FCNL, I was introduced to new ways of thinking about my own spiritual condition, of understanding God's presence in my life. One of these ways has been through spiritual friendships. That's how I think of Debbie Humphries — as a spiritual Friend — both to me and many others. We spent many hours on walks and talks as well as in corporate worship in Hartford Monthly Meeting. I came to know Debbie as a seeker and a scientist. She deeply values the faith and practices of Quakerism — skills available for all spiritual seekers.

Debbie's curiosity and persistent practice of personal discernment and corporate discernment have helped me understand the power of Quakerism to help us listen to the Life within us and to influence the world around us. This capacity to be both contemplative and active, to search for truth in ourselves and others and to call it out — this is what makes Quaker practice so valuable and so sorely needed in the world today.

Diane Randall, Executive Secretary
Friends Committee on National Legislation

Introduction

I GREW UP MORMON and came to Quakerism as an adult in my mid-twenties. As a child, I sang songs, prayed in Sunday School each week, and had lessons about topics such as honesty, honoring my parents, and humility. Messages from church adults about practices such as telling the truth, respecting others, and saying my prayers supported the teachings of my parents. I took these admonitions to heart, saying my prayers in the morning and at night, kneeling by my bedside. We were encouraged to work at being better people. I learned songs like "Jesus Wants me for a Sunbeam" and "I am a Child of God," which shaped my childhood and my understanding of God. Friends from church were at the center of my family's community.

As I grew older, I became more aware of some of the cultural currents surrounding participation in organized religions, particularly among intellectuals and people who considered themselves politically or socially liberal or progressive. "I'm deeply spiritual, but not religious" is a statement I've heard from the young adults I work with in my professional life, and I've read it in books and articles about today's religious culture. It is a common refrain. It's a statement that has always jarred me; something about it seems a bit off. I have walked with the phrase for some time, seeking to understand why I have discomfort with its premise. The clarity I eventually came to is that it is far easier to see myself as a deeply spiritual and good person when I'm not engaged with a religious community and the real-life challenges of learning to love those with whom I disagree. I find participation in a religious tradition an essential element of accountability and encouragement, an important place for checking discernment, and an essential laboratory for building a beloved community. We need places where we can be our flawed, genuine, human selves, where we are accepted and still encouraged to challenge ourselves to do better. For me, talking with others, sharing goals with family or friends, and having others encourage me on my spiritual journey is an important part of challenging myself to a deeper spirituality and a life that witnesses to my faith. In addition to account-ability and encouragement, a religious community can also be a source of feedback on our journeys. Sometimes, when I listen to God, I'm not sure whether I'm hearing my own echo chamber of wishes and delusions. Having others who will listen with me and to whom I will listen is another important part of spiritual growth.

As a child and adolescent I studied the history of Mormonism, and I internalized the truth of Joseph Smith's story of the founding of the Mormon Church as a restoration of primitive Christianity. As an adult in my mid-twenties, I came to Quakerism, and the first time I read George Fox's *Journal* I was struck by the parallels. The origin stories of Quakerism and Mormonism are very similar — a young man on a spiritual quest trying to hear what God wants him to do, and using deep reading of the Bible to understand how God works in the world. Both George Fox (England, 1640s) and Joseph Smith (Vermont, USA, 1820s) were looking for a religious experience with the vitality and power of the Spirit they read about in the Bible. George Fox travelled around England, visiting ministers and asking for their advice. He concluded they were talking about and preaching a level of experi-ence with the living God they themselves did not possess. Joseph Smith went to the revival meetings and listened to the ministers of the different denominations, each claiming they had the truth and that people needed to join *their* church to be saved. Both Joseph and George were eventually led to ask God directly for guidance, and each had a transformative experience of the Divine in response. From that transformative experience, each went on to found a unique Christian community, and both claimed to restore primitive Christianity.

As an adult, I was able to hear and accept the validity and power of each of these experiences. As I held my awareness of the origin stories of both Mormonism and Quakerism as true, I was led to listen deeply for the interaction between the human and the Divine at the foundation of other religious traditions. When reading the Koran and Karen Armstrong's book on Mohammed,[1] I was struck with the parallels there also — a young man looking for and finding God. Although the originating experiences as described by each feel deeply true, my experience is that a profoundly human structure gets built

1 Karen Armstrong, *Muhammad: A Biography of the Prophet* (San Francisco: HarperOne, 1993).

on such experiences, and sometimes the human structures get in the way of our living into the guidance of the Divine Spirit.

For my part, I believe each of the religious traditions in the world has a unique contribution to make, growing out of a specific time and place, yet rooted in eternal truths. I seek to understand the potential and the uniqueness of each tradition. I ask, *What viewpoint or understanding does the constellation of beliefs and practices of a particular religious tradition bring?* When I ask this question, it's not about how the tradition is being practiced today. It is much more about the potential of the tradition — what could the tradition offer if fully lived? Another way of expressing my understanding is with a metaphor of the Divine River, to which each tradition, at its best, guides believers. Along the Divine River, each tradition has its own unique beach.

In tending the Quaker beach, I have actively engaged with the broader network of Quakers. More of my journey among Quakers is shared in the pages below, but the rough outline is that I first worshiped with Quakers in Cairo, Egypt during the first Gulf War (1990–91), and became a member five years later in Ithaca Monthly Meeting, New York Yearly Meeting (May 1995).[2] I then transferred membership to Charleston Monthly Meeting (West Virginia) in the Southern Appalachian Yearly Meeting and Association when my family and I moved to West Virginia in June 1995. When my family and I moved to Connecticut in 1998, we transferred our membership to Hartford Monthly Meeting in New England Yearly Meeting. I have worshiped with Quakers in North and South America, Europe, Africa, the Middle East, and Asia. I have served on committees of my monthly and yearly meeting, and on committees of wider Quaker organizations such as School of the Spirit Ministries, American Friends Service Committee, and Friends World Committee for Consultation. I have travelled in the ministry and worshiped with Friends from a range of perspectives — evangelical, liberal, orthodox, conservative. I have been troubled for years by the question of what the Quaker peace testimony stands for when we are unable to get along in our own monthly, quarterly and yearly meeting communities. The historical

---

2 Quaker congregations are organized into a nested community, from local congregations that meet to conduct business on a monthly schedule (monthly meetings), to regional meetings that conduct business quarterly (quarterly meetings), and larger regional meetings that conduct business annually (yearly meetings).

(and ongoing) splits and divisions in Quakerism are to me a painful sign that Quakers are less as a people than we are called to be.

Quakerism is grounded in communion with the Divine and holds in tension with the grace of that communion the importance of developing and honing skills of tuning, listening, discerning, translating and testing our alignment with the Divine. The skill-building is encouraged first at the individual level and then at the community level. Quakerism focuses less on the content of one's beliefs and more on practice. We have a tradition that can transform lives so that those lives live more deeply in Spirit. While these practices are not necessarily unique to Quakerism, the Quaker tradition caries a gestalt of belief, practice and structure. At our best, we know that the act of loving another person is more important than what that person believes, and this understanding is integrated into our shared practices. Quaker corporate discernment,[3] with its measured flow and careful listening, allows space for holding paradox and ambiguity. The structure of Quaker religious communities has a limited hierarchy with little formal authority vested in specific individuals. My experience is that the Quaker path is unique because of the belief in grounding our lives and actions in love, in corporate practices that focus on listening deeply, and in a structure that limits the accumulation of individual power.

One of the needed fruits of the Quaker path is the tradition of listening together. Quakerism is rooted in listening to each other and to the Spirit. Corporate skills are about putting the shared listening and discernment into action. This skill of listening along with others to how the Spirit is moving builds on the foundation of personal spiritual practices. Participation in corporate worship, where we listen for the movement of the Spirit, is open even to individuals with no personal spiritual practices. However, the depth of the shared worship and the ease of listening together does rely on some of those present coming prepared, having spent time during the week in their own spiritual listening. Similarly, for corporate discernment to work, each person present needs to be able to discern the difference between their own notions and willfulness and the promptings of the still, small voice Quakers refer to as Spirit or Inner Light. Can we listen and name

3 Quakers speak of corporate discernment and corporate worship drawing on the Latin root of *corpus*, to refer to the community as a single body.

when we feel the Presence guiding us or others, and when we do not? Can we remain silent until the Holy Spirit fills our hearts and guides our words? There are great potential fruits of this practice if we can become fluent enough to walk with it in our daily lives. We need to be more faithful in our waiting and our listening so we speak from the spirit of love and truth in our everyday lives. Quaker practices all cluster together to help tune to the frequency of the Spirit, to listen deeply, and to be able to discern when we are individually and corporately tuned so we are hearing the guidance of the Inward Teacher.

The essays in the first section of this book draw on my own experiences of working with these practices, focusing on personal spiritual practices and my experience of leaving one religious tradition for another. Personal spiritual practices are how we learn to tune to the Inward Teacher, Inner Light, or Inner Christ — and to discern when we are in tune and when we are not. Quakerism, with its emphasis on the possibility of the unmediated experience of the Divine, relies on the skill of tuning to the Divine frequency. It takes practice to be able to open to and hone in on the frequency consistently, rapidly, and smoothly. The first essay, "Soul Time," speaks to my primary spiritual practice through the years of morning listening, and is about making regular space for listening in my life. Once we recognize the experience of being in tune, then we practice reproducing and refining that experience. The second essay, "Finding Support," reflects on how I have found companionship and encouragement as I live with a call to ministry among Friends. The third essay, "Being Clear," describes some of my efforts to practice deep listening for the Spirit in my daily life. There was a time some nine years into my journey with Friends when I realized that I could only be sure that I was in tune if I was in worship and being moved to speak. Over the following year I took monthly personal retreats to practice listening and tuning, so I could come to know and name the feeling of Spirit in my daily life. That journey is described in the fourth essay in this section, "A Listening Year." "From Mormon to Quaker," first drafted in the early 2000s when I was in my late thirties, speaks to the challenge of listening for and respecting the gifts of different religious traditions through the lens of my own experience leaving Mormonism. It also frames the fundamental question I walk with, of what is culture and what is truth, and how to better see truth.

The second section includes essays on a number of topics. Each one speaks in some way to the quote Margaret Fell remembered George Fox saying when she first heard him preach, "What canst thou say?" These essays all speak to my understanding of Truth from my walk with the Inward Teacher. "Our Hope for a New Life," reflections on the Apostle Paul's teachings about the resurrection, came as a gift when I was taking course, Introduction to preaching, at Earlham School of Religion. "Grafting in" is an interweaving of my Mormon heritage and the Quaker tradition with the image of grafting, using a parable from the Book of Mormon and quotations from the Bible and early Friends. Using the metaphor of grafting, I offer an invitation to each of us to attend to whether we are being fruitful where we are, and to more fully engage with the roots of our faith. "Engaging with a Monthly Meeting," co-authored with Diane Randall, shares the journey of my own monthly meeting when faced with my call to ministry. "The Four Pillars of Meeting for Business" shares my understanding of the core elements of Quaker business practice. "Embracing Wholeness" interweaves scripture, metaphor, and stories to explore the concept of wholeness in a talk given at a liberal Mormon women's gathering. "The Unwritten Rules of Waiting Worship" shares my reflections on Quaker worship. In worship Quakers seek to merge our individual experiences of opening, tuning and attending to the Divine into a shared experience of listening. "The Lies I Live" shares my ongoing exploration of the colonization of our world by a worldview that is antithetical to the wellbeing of humans and the entire planetary system, and the ways in which my daily life is based on the foundational lies of this invasive worldview. The final essay in this section, "Why the World Needs Quakerism," explores in more depth the three elements of belief, practice, and structure that I see at the core of the promise of Quakerism, and how those elements could be transformative to individuals and the world as a whole.

The essays that are included here share my journey into Quakerism, first with the spiritual practices that have nourished me, and then moving into my own growing understanding of the amazing potential of the Quaker path. Embedded throughout is my sense that each religious tradition embodies a unique path to the river of Divine Life, a path where some individuals will flourish. The multiplicity of traditions around the world is essential for allowing each human being to find the tradition that nurtures and supports their journey with truth. My hope is that this book will be of use to spiritual seekers with no relationship to the Religious Society of Friends as well as to those who have walked with the Religious Society of Friends for some time. To that end, there is a glossary of some Quaker terminology, which I hope will be of use.

Please read "as led," whether straight through, dipping in and out of different essays, or reading one or more and then stopping. My hope in sharing these essays is to invite others to dive more fully into the spiritual practices of Quakerism and other faith traditions. By sharing my lived experience of the challenge, rigor and relevance of the principles and practices of Quakerism today, I pray that others may find themselves led to fully embrace the challenge of living into their own faith tradition.

SECTION 1

*Spiritual Practice
and Development*

The essays in this section describe different stages and components of my spiritual journey, focusing on the practical skills of tuning, listening, discernment and how I've found support and companionship on my journey. Development by individuals of the skills of tuning, listening and discernment is foundational to the Quaker practice of corporate discernment. My experience of Quaker congregations today is that much of the spiritual growth of members relies on self-directed learning, and independent seeking. This section describes my own learning process as I have sought to practice the promise of Quakerism today.

CHAPTER 1

Soul Time

"I DON'T HAVE THE TIME." "I can't, I'm too busy." "I just can't get everything done." We say and hear comments like these all the time. But what is it that we really don't have time for? We spend time developing our bodies and minds, but I propose that we need more time developing our souls. We need *soul time*, time with our deeper selves, to learn and grow. We need time outside of regular time so that when we come back, we have greater perspective about our pace, aspirations, and priorities. When we take soul time, we eventually realize that all our achievements, no matter how prestigious, are nothing in comparison to the depth and timing of our souls.

So what does "soul time" look like? You know it when you have it. I struggle to find it consistently. Sometimes I can get there through meditation. Other times it's watching a fire, gardening or hand sewing. Sometimes I find it in Meeting for Worship or playing with children. I have about an hour every morning that I designate as Soul Time. I read, write and worship. And then through the rest of the day I try to slip in brief pauses of worship to refresh my soul.

There's a mix of personal effort and personal preparedness involved in my methods. In *Our Greatest Gift*[1] Henri Nouwen writes about getting to know a family of trapeze artists. One of the key lessons he learned is that there are different roles, most particularly the role of the flyer and the role of the catcher. I keep remembering that the flyer must not ever catch the catcher. I hear this in a certain way: the flyers need to jump, put their arms or body in the agreed upon place, and trust that they will be caught, just as we must let go and let the Spirit catch us. If the flyer tries to grab for the catcher, the flyer will likely fall. The flyer's role requires significant preparation and readiness to be in the right place, and in position to be caught, but once they jump, it is up to the catcher.

---

1 Henri J. M. Nouwen, *Our Greatest Gift: A Meditation on Dying and Caring* (San Francisco: HarperOne, 1994).

Sitting

When my boys were little, they'd get up in the mornings and come down and cuddle with me on the couch under the quilt. The quilt we wrapped up in then was a red gingham cotton that my sister Vixie gave me one Christmas. It had a printed top with a pattern of pseudo quilt squares that she had tied with yarn. When the quilt disintegrated, assisted on its journey by small hands using scissors to cut tufts of yarn, I found another printed cotton fabric to make a replacement.

The new quilt has images of birds, each in its own square — a bluebird, robin, sparrow and chickadee, repeated across the top. I tied the quilt with yarn as Vixie had, even though all the other quilts I've made are hand quilted, with rows of small stitches in patterns across the quilt to hold the batting in place. The couch quilt, with the top just two long pieces of patterned fabric sewn together in the middle, didn't get that detailed treatment. It was a rush job, something to finish. And yet it is more present in my daily life than any of the other quilts I've made.

When I sit in the mornings, I want to be under cover. Even in the hot summer mornings, I'll wrap my legs in the cool cotton, loving the feel of the smooth fabric. When I'm not at home I look for a cover of some kind to wrap around me in the mornings. I don't know why. I can imagine psychological interpretations both positive and negative. Perhaps it's a sign of humility, aligned with those religious traditions where you do not go uncovered before God. Perhaps it's a protective barrier or shield, a refusal to be completely open to the spirit. Or it could just a complex mixture of both. I've sheltered under many coverings in my years of morning listening — fine woven throws, treasured quilts, hand knit afghans, light blankets and down comforters. Under those covers I sit cross legged or sprawled, or often with my knees to my chest. I don't worry about position, or what I do. It's really just about being there.

Sometimes my Soul Time is taken up with pre-occupations with work, and I'll get my to-do list out and leave it to make notes on, so I can put down the worries and obsessions and come back to breathing deep into my core. The breathing seems to go somewhere in the center of my pelvis, just drawing the breath in and filling the space. Trying to breathe into the torso, I hold my consciousness and focus in

December 2010

For months I've been feeling a pull/concern to spend time just sitting in our backyard. And I finally started doing it a couple of weeks ago — sitting against one particular tree, watching the trees, birds, squirrels and cats.

July 2014

I'm sitting in the backyard with my back against the tree. Lots of birds this morning, several in pairs. I think I saw a pair of purple finches — first the male and then the female land on the end of a long, spindly dead branch. It was one of the lowest (at close to 20 feet) branches coming off a split trunk/two trunk maple. I just lay down on the picnic table CJ and John turned into a bench for me one Mother's Day. Lying down I can look up through the branches and leaves of the four trees that are clustered here. Looking up the layers of leaves have slightly different colors, perhaps due to the light and wind.

October 2016

Sitting in the pavilion [that my husband John built in the summer of 2016] with the roof overhead feels so different from sitting at the base of one of the trees. I sit in a human space, where I can feel completely at home. It's a functional outdoor living space, and with the hugelkulture [an old German wood-composting technique] mound in front of it there is a sense of seclusion, despite the visibility of 16–17 other houses. There's something about the finished wooden floor, where I'm not worried about getting my blanket all dirty, and the roof overhead that together provide an intangible feeling of shelter. This is my space, in the middle of the garden.

the same deeply internal place. Sometimes I sit with a particular question — *How do I respond to X?*, with X representing intrapersonal dilemmas, work challenges, family challenges, or any place in my life where I'm not quite sure of the best way forward. And generally, if I sit long enough, some insight comes that helps me do something or say something that moves the situation in a positive way. Sometimes I'll come to a session of sitting full of anxieties and worries, and I need to sit there until I feel more open and settled. The release can come almost instantaneously, after an extended period of drifting toward that deeper centered space.

For years I sat inside, and then a few more years I sat outside sporadically, sometimes on the ground on a pad or log leaning against a tree, or on a bench against a tree. Finally, in December 2010 I was able to make the shift to more regularly sitting outside. Sitting outside is very different from sitting inside. Inside it is about listening internally. Outside it's about listening externally, and hearing the life and vitality of the Spirit in the vibrant world around me.

Other Practices

While sitting has been my principal practice through the years, there have been times I experimented with other practices. After a visit to Bhutan in March 2016 I spent four months doing 100 full prostrations every morning, until I reached 10,000, and then I was clear to stop. What I still keep from the experiment is the practice of taking refuge, which I use for centering myself, and sometimes for quieting my mind for sleep.

I take refuge in the Light
I take refuge in the wisdom
I take refuge in the great cloud of witnesses

Benefits of Soul Time

There's an apocryphal story attributed to Martin Luther (and others). He said that when he had the most to do, he had to pray for four hours a day to get everything done. The Dalai Lama's regular morning prayers take four hours, and he rises at 4:30 AM to fit them into his day.[2] There's an epistle from Ireland Half-Yearly Quaker Meeting in 1676 that tells of spending two days in meeting for worship, trying multiple times to shift to the business agenda, but each time finding those gathered called by the Spirit back into meeting for worship. Finally, on the morning of the third day, they shifted smoothly into their business

2 His Holiness the Dalai Lama and Howard C. Cutler, *The Art of Happiness: A Handbook for Living* (London: Penguin Books Ltd, 1998).

6

session.[3] One of the clearest benefits of this much soul time is that you end up in a state where you're very calm but full of energy.

We've all known times when we calmly accomplished more than we thought we could — days when we just seemed to breeze through tasks. Now there's research that documents the productivity of states of calm energy. Undergraduate subjects did their best studying by far in states of calm energy. Robert Thayer has studied moods for the last fifteen years, and has identified two states, energy and tension, which he sees as the foundation underlying our moods. We all feel some combination of tension and energy. Calm energy is the most productive state for studying, tense energy is next, followed by calm tiredness, and then tense tiredness. Thayer also found that meditation or prayer reduces tension and helps to turn tense energy into calm energy or tense tiredness into calm tiredness.[4]

Another benefit of soul time is that priorities are restructured. We evaluate our activities for their service to our souls with the possibility of dropping unnecessary activities. John Woolman struggled to keep his activities limited in order to develop his relationship with God. "The increase of business became my burthen, for though my natural inclination was towards merchandise, yet I believed Truth required me to live more free from outward cumbers."[5] We need to say no to good activities that are not right for us. We, like John Woolman, must use the yardstick of what Truth requires of us as we plan our daily schedules. What good, but less "right" activities are we engaged in that are weighing us down with "outward cumbers?"

Making Soul Time

One of the keys to having enough of anything is believing that you have enough. And this is also true of time. Have faith that the

3 Thomas Wight and John Rutty, *A history of the rise and progress of the people called Quakers in Ireland : from the year 1653 to 1700*, 4th Edition (1811), p. 129. Digital Quaker Collection, Earlham School of Religion. http://dqc.esr.earlham.edu:8080/xmlmm/loginB?XMLMMToc=E4662571&XMLMMLanguage=English&XMLMMCollection=/earlham&XMLMMReturnURL=http://www.qhpress.org/cgi-bin/catalog.cgi%3Fname%3Dthomas.wight

4 Stephen Kiesling, "Beyond the Good, the Bad, and the Ugly," *Spirituality and Health* (Fall 1999).

5 John Woolman, *The Journal and Major Essays of John Woolman*, edited by Phillips P. Moulton (Richmond, Indiana: Friends United Press, 1989), p. 53.

combination of an increase in productivity and a decrease in unnecessary activities will give you as much Soul Time as you need. And if you watch, there are opportunities for Soul Time everywhere. Thich Nhat Hanh has written extensively on integrating Soul Time into our daily lives with ideas such as seeing the Buddha's eyes in the tail lights of cars in front of us on the road.

Queries

What spiritual practices have nourished you?

Are there spiritual practices you are drawn to try?

What gets in the way of your making regular soul time?

CHAPTER 2

Finding Support for a Call to Ministry

IN AUGUST 1999 I HAD A TRANSFORMATIONAL EXPERIENCE that was a powerful call to ministry. The call is described in Chapter 8, "Engaging with a Monthly Meeting,"[1] so I'll just say here that others in the yearly meeting and my monthly meeting knew that "something" had happened to me.

The following spring, Diane Randall, from the Hartford Monthly Meeting Worship and Ministry Committee, asked both my husband John and me to consider attending a workshop called "Emerging Ministries" being offered by New England Yearly Meeting Ministry and Counsel. We were both clear to go, and John's mother Judy was able to come up from Tennessee to stay with our sons, who were three and five years old.

We drove up the steep hill of Keets Road for the Emerging Ministries retreat and arrived at the conference center and cabins at the end of the road, with the forested hills to the west and the trees down the meadow to the east. We gathered after dinner Friday night in the small affinity groups that would be the center of much of our experience over the weekend. We were each invited to name the ministry that was emerging in us, and the words that came out for me were that I was being called to the traditional Quaker ministry of travel and speaking. On Saturday Charlotte Fardelmann led a mentoring and guided meditation exercise. In my journal I describe this experience:

> Charlotte led the visualization, and before we did the visualization she had us write down mentors and three characteristics that drew us to the mentors. I wrote down George Fox, John Woolman, Eleanor Godway and John Punshon. The three characteristics I

1 My call to ministry is also described in a Pendle Hill Pamphlet, *Spreading the Fire: Encouraging Friends through Travel in the Ministry*, Pendle Hill Pamphlet #436 (Wallingford, PA: Pendle Hill, 2015).

noted were passion for depth, love of all life, and striving to live with integrity. Then Charlotte told us that we were drawn to these characteristics in others because they were arising within ourselves.

The next part of the exercise was to get comfortable, so I lay down on the floor. She guided us to imagine going down a country road, seeing a path off into the woods, taking the path and eventually coming to a large meadow. She told us to start across the meadow and find a stream through the center, then stop at the stream and sit down. She asked us to envision the mentor coming out of the woods across the stream. For me, four figures came out of the woods, but the name I put with the figure that crossed the stream was George Fox. I felt like sobbing when that happened. The visualization continued with instructions about asking specific questions and listening to the replies. The question I remember asking was "How do I know when I'm on the right path?" And I don't remember the answer. But then we were told that the mentor gave us a gift. And George Fox gave me a ball, a liahona. Out of Mormon tradition, it's a compass or pathfinder that works according to the faith and righteousness of the people (Journal, April 2000).

For our Sunday morning closing small group activity, we took turns sitting in a chair for what was called "worship seeing." We laid our hands on the person in the chair, and out of worship, each shared what we saw emerging in the focus person. When it was my turn to sit in the chair, Sirkka Barbour said that she saw a female prophet crying in the wilderness. I was in tears for most of the activity, feeling both the affirmation of being called out, and also humbled by the call. The Emerging Ministries retreat was a foundational experience of support and affirmation for me, encouraging and challenging me to take my spiritual growth and the nascent call to ministry seriously.

Brian Drayton, a recorded Quaker minister in New Hampshire, talks about acute and chronic leadings to ministry. As I understand him, acute experiences are the upwelling and bursting forth of ministry through an individual at a unique point in time. Chronic experiences are when an individual has repeated experiences of the upwelling of the Spirit into ministry. There are parallels to the kinds of support I've found through the years. Experiences such as the naming of my gift, and the encouragement to accept and live up to it I experienced at the Emerging Ministries retreat are acute support, where there is encouragement and affirmation at a single point in time. The support committee I've had for the last sixteen years is an example of chronic support. Within the categories of both acute and chronic support are a range of sources of support — Quaker friends, family, readings, personal meditation, and specific spiritual practices.

I have been blessed to travel with wonderful mentors and teachers. Early in my journey I agreed to serve on the newly formed Faith and Practice Revision Committee of New England Yearly Meeting. Jan Hoffman, a Quaker with extensive experience of ministry and eldering, was clerking the committee. She lived an hour from me, so I would often drive to her place the night before so I could get a good night's sleep and drive with her the next morning. Those rides together were a gift, and a very important monthly source of encouragement and support for the three years I served on that committee. Through those conversations I heard Jan's teaching stories, as she shared some of her experiences of traveling in the ministry. I was also able to share my experiences and reflections and to hear Jan's reactions and encouragement.

Support Committee

The first part of finding chronic support was acknowledging my need. Shortly after the Emerging Ministries retreat I asked a few seasoned Friends from Hartford Monthly Meeting (HMM) to sit with me on a regular basis, to form an informal support committee. I spoke with Diane Randall, who was serving as clerk (see glossary) of Hartford Meeting at the time, to see if she had suggestions of names. Developing that committee involved multiple conversations where I tried to explain my sense of need. I explained that at the Emerging Ministries retreat it had become fairly clear that the ministry I was feeling called to was the traditional Quaker ministry of speaking and travel. To be faithful to the call, I needed feedback and guidance — suggestions of things to do, a place to share the fears and concerns I had as I worked to allow this ministry to emerge. One of those seasoned Friends, Eleanor Godway, was particularly helpful in setting up the support committee, reaching out for multiple conversations. The Friends I approached were somewhat puzzled by the request, as it was not something Hartford Meeting was in the habit of doing. The first time we met I told them I needed help making sure I wasn't running ahead or behind my leading. We started meeting in late summer of 2000, and I continue meeting monthly with a support committee to this day.

For each meeting I write a short one to two page report. We begin with centering worship, and then members of my support committee do a short check-in of their own lives, with updates on family, work or other activities. Following their check-in, they may ask questions about what was in or not in my report, or they ask me to share more. The listening and offering of *queries* (see glossary) and reflections is often the most valuable part of our meetings. Sometimes I speak very matter-of-factly and rationally, and the committee reminds me to listen for the life and excitement that is one of the hallmarks of the moving of the Spirit. Sometimes I use a language of 'shoulds,' and the committee will remind me to try to release the 'shoulds,' which often represent cultural expectations, and instead to listen for the deeper invitation. One of the gifts of a support or oversight committee like this is that they are helping individuals hear and follow their own call to ministry. Thus the work of this committee stays focused on drawing out the ministry. Eleanor Godway, in her introduction to a talk I gave at Beacon Hill Friends House in Boston, described her sense of how accompanying me had affected her and others:

> The experience of being part of this committee [the support committee] helped me understand how helping test someone's leading involved us all in that leading. It becomes a leading which is known to be a leading not just for Debbie but for us, in the committee, and for Hartford Meeting as it found clearness over several years to endorse a travel minute for her. And then it becomes a leading that the Quarter is involved in, and in due course, as we take it further, New England Yearly Meeting as well. It becomes a leading for Friends everywhere.[2]

Friends and Family

Both John and my extended families have been important sources of periodic support and encouragement. Our mothers were able to

2 Eleanor Godway, in the introduction to Debbie Humphries' *Listen! Series* pamphlet, *On Being Grafted Into the Root* (Boston, MA: Beacon Hill Friends House, Spring 2008).

come from Utah and Tennessee several times to stay with our sons so we could participate in different retreats and workshops. The Hogue Rodleys, in Cambridge, Massachusetts, provided a home away from home for our sons for years, freeing both John and me to serve regularly on New England Yearly Meeting committees. When our sons were young, Jennifer Hogue shared the story of being asked by Anne Kriebel from the New England Yearly Meeting Nominating Committee what she was doing to support the yearly meeting. Jennifer's response was that she was taking care of the Humphries' boys so John and Debbie could serve on committees, and Anne thanked her and agreed that it was important service.

Regular conversations and walks with friends have been essential supports, allowing me to share ideas, reflections and experiences. At the Friends World Committee for Consultation Section of the Americas meeting in March 2017, Chuck Schobert and I walked around and around the circle drive in the middle of Stony Point Center almost every evening, sharing our spiritual journeys and challenges.

Peak Experiences

The Emerging Ministries retreat, and the naming of my gift by Sirkka Barbour, was an experience of acute support that nourished me for quite awhile. A year or so afterward, when I heard about the invitation-only Friends General Conference (FGC) traveling ministries retreat, I was clear to contact Michael Wajda, development director for FGC, who I had met at New England Yearly Meeting sessions when he was an FGC visitor, to ask if I should reach out about an invitation. He encouraged me to do so, and my participation in those retreats for a number of years was an important source of periodic support. Through those retreats I also built relationships with Friends outside New England Yearly Meeting, who I can still reach out to today if needed.

Participating in, and leading, workshops has also an been important source of support, where I received both insights and encouragement. One example is from late spring 2002, when Hartford Meeting was engaging with my request for oversight of my ministry. Charlotte Fardelmann had driven down from her home in Portsmouth,

New Hampshire to offer a workshop on leadings. We sat together in the Williams Room at Hartford meeting in a small group of maybe ten to twelve people. For this exercise, Charlotte gently led us through a guided meditation culminating in an invitation to listen for a word or image of what was nudging each of us. The image that erupted, through deep emotion and near sobs, was that I was to be a mouthpiece — a connection for the spirit to blow through. This image revealed that Spirit blows through me, into the traditions and things that many of us know, which gives shape to the sound each of us hears. To do this I needed to know the traditions, and I needed to know the Spirit that blows. My gift/leading would be raucous noise if it was not attached to a community (the horn itself). And the community had to own the gift. This image has stayed with me, accentuating the importance of the connections both to the tradition of Quakerism and to the living community.

One dream, from Jan 2002, while a single experience, has been another important source of encouragement and support. In the dream I experienced having a new job which I wasn't sure I could do. I was taken to meet a couple of people traveling by ferry to another point of land. At the second place I was shown a building and some land and given a piece of paper with phone numbers for people I was to call about the building and land. The next day I went to the main office where I met the head of the office, the Princess of Peace. She was doing a benefit performance at the office, and I met lots of people while things got set up. I wondered if I was supposed to be there or if I should be off making the calls. The princess looked at me quizzically a couple of times, as if to say "Why are you here?" I helped pass out song sheets to make myself useful. The show culminated with the Princess of Peace processing into the auditorium dressed in a simple white gown with gold trim, Mars coming out from behind the curtains on the stage, and the two of them playing ping pong. At this point I realized that my work was not the ping pong match between war and peace, but instead the land on the other side of the river. I lost my place in the packed hall, along with the paper with phone numbers. I left the office and the dream ended with me wandering through deserted streets of a post-apocalyptic city, having lost the paper with the numbers, and not knowing what to do next.

Sitting in Quaker worship a few days later, a sense of invitation washed over me that I was invited to describe and help claim the place we need to go as a global human community. This was a liberation, a freeing, through the early years of the Second Iraq War, to not need to follow the ping pong match between war and peace. Other themes I've drawn from the dream over the years are that I got diverted from my main task. The song sheets were a reminder that my desire to be helpful and the tendency to say yes to concrete immediate needs may sometimes distract me from my real work. In getting diverted from my main task, there is always the danger that I am letting go of the things I need to pursue my primary work.

During the mid-2000s I periodically visited an energy healer named Kathy LeDonne. Right before my first opportunity to lead a workshop with Peter Crysdale on *Deepening the Silence and Inviting Vital Ministry*, I had a visit with Kathy. After some minutes of work she said she had something she needed to say. She said it was not her usual practice, but the words had come three times, which was her signal to listen. What she shared was a gift: "I charge you with my words. Let this be a gift, and not a burden. You were made for this." And then she made me say three times, "I surrender my ego to your will; I will lift up your words."

Each of these peak experiences came at a time when I needed the encouragement. They have stayed with me to provide nourishment and affirmation in dry periods. Each experience has served as a touchstone through the years.

Personal Listening

Personal spiritual practices are at the core of my own support system. Passages from specific books, personal worship, the I Ching, writing with my non-dominant hand, and more recently, the Transformation Game, have all provided encouragement and support.

> I took the quilt to meeting for business on Sunday to work on it. Some concern about appearing to show off. Samuel Bownas' book on *A Description of the Qualifications of a Gospel Minister* talks of all the things that can subvert the message of the Spirit, including fear of those present. And I know that frequently my awareness of

those present does make me worry about how what I say will be received. And at the Emerging Ministries retreat I made an unconscious decision to trust the people there. And so I spoke without thinking about the effects of what I said. And because I was not thinking or worrying about how people would receive what I said, I was able to speak from a very deep place. And it's a place I want to be in more. (Journal, May 2000)

I walked with my over-concern for the expectations of others for years, holding the knowledge that I needed to release expectations to more fully allow the Spirit to come through.

When I had spoken to Lucy Townsend on Friday, the process we've followed, both of my asking and the meeting considering the request for oversight had felt so right. And then all of the sudden Sunday afternoon I was plunged into a place of dis-ease. I was unsettled, and not really sure why. I ended up sitting in the chair in our bedroom for almost two hours, dozing a bit at first and then just sitting. Periodically I would check to see if there was energy around any of the other activities that came to mind, and finally a little after 4 PM I got up and put the boxes of clothes away I had taken out for the boys. (Journal, April 2002)

Time after time through the years I've ended up sitting until I found that place of calm.

Some years ago, Michael Wajda shared a tool he had heard of, writing a question with your dominant hand and then writing the answer with the non-dominant hand. I have used this approach a few times through the years. A few examples from my journals:

What am I supposed to be listening for and what is the best way to listen?

Left handed: Listen for a voice that is both yours and not yours. Listen everywhere, but make time and space to listen alone and outside. Make spaces in your day — even five minute breaks — to sink down to that well. When you are doing "mindless" work breathe deeply and listen. I am everywhere. (Journal, August 2000)

What am I called to do right now? Today? Over the next few months?

Left handed: Intentions must become action. You have intentions with many things — things close to home, where you can learn readily to become action. The computer can suck the intentions up so that you forget your purpose. Choose to use it wisely. (Journal, May 2002)

God, I ask for a blessing to take me in this next phase of my life.

Left handed: I bless you with joy — a joy of abundance. You will have challenging work in a supportive environment, joyful time with your sons, and the safety and security and surety of a husband who loves you. Your home will welcome all who come there, and will be a place of rest and peace. (Journal, May 2005)

The Transformation Game was in the games closet at Woolman Hill, a Quaker conference center in Deerfield, Massachusetts, when I was there for a Connecticut Valley Quarterly Meeting gathering in October 2012. I remember pulling it out and making fun of it with Margaret Cooley. But something stuck with me, and when I looked it up and found that it had been developed by the Findhorn Community in Scotland, I ordered the game online. You play the game holding a specific question, your playing focus, and then roll the dice to fill your personal unconscious envelope with setbacks, angels and insights. You roll the dice to move along your life path, working through the physical, mental, emotional and spiritual levels while clearing your unconscious envelope. I have played the game with numerous friends and family members, finding insights and encouragement in the "random" cards that come.

Sample Transformation Game Focus Questions:

How do I open my heart more fully? (September 2013)

How do I release my own internal competitiveness/envy of others? (November 2013)

What are my next steps in releasing myself to be more obedient to the Spirit? (May 2014)

My support has come from an eclectic mix of directions, and I offer them as examples and suggestions of things you might consider for yourself. As you look for your own support, I encourage you to remember an old Russian proverb — trust, but verify. Trust your own knowing, and find others who can listen with you, to help you regularly calibrate your listening to verify that you are listening to the Inward Teacher.

Queries

When have I felt most free to share honestly and deeply with others about my own spiritual journey?

What do I do when I feel most alone? Do I balance seeking support and guidance from F/friends and loved ones with seeking support and guidance from the Inward Teacher?

When have I felt most encouraged and supported in my spiritual journey?

CHAPTER 3

Being Clear — Feeling My Way through Life

WHEN SOMETHING DOESN'T FEEL LIKE AN IMPORTANT DECISION when I pause to listen, I move forward with whatever my own inclination is. Other times I hold a question of whether to take a particular step for months before I'm clear on how to move forward. In May 2002 I got the 2002–3 Pendle Hill catalog and found two week-long courses I was very intrigued by, offered back to back in February 2003. I sat for months with the question of whether to register for one or both workshops. I wanted to spend time with Bill Taber, who was leading one of them. But I kept thinking about the time it would take and the burden on my family from me being gone for so long. I was never clear whether I should pick up the phone and call Pendle Hill. Finally my support committee reminded me that other times I had felt clear about moving forward with a specific endeavor, so I let go of the idea of attending the Pendle Hill workshop. Letting go of that option opened the way for me to consider other possibilities, and on the drive home from a conference in Washington, D.C., I reflected on the possibility of going to Barnesville, Ohio. The next day I was clear to call Bill and Fran Taber and set up a time to travel to Barnesville to stay at the Quaker retreat center there for a few days.

Discernment for me is a process of listening, of holding different options up to the Light and sensing how I feel. Sometimes I only have one option to hold up; other times there are several. Most times the answer does not come as quickly as I would like it to. As I wait for clarity on particular questions, I listen both in my morning time and during the day to see if I can get any hints or help. Being clear for me is a feeling of rightness. Sometimes it is a faint pull in a particular direction, such as a willingness to go shopping at a Nordstrom's outlet with my sister-in-law, something I would not normally do. Other times it is a ringing clarity, like when I sat with the question of whether to serve on the New England Yearly Meeting Faith and

Practice Revision Committee and got the answer to take up this task with joy. I don't always pause to listen, and I don't always follow the guidance when it comes. But that is what I work toward — listening at all times, and following as led.

Jonathan Vogel-Borne is one of my fellow travelers in ministry, co-leading Friends General Conference Gathering and Powell House[1] workshops. Early on as we started working together he drew my attention to how I used language of both "walking with" and "sitting with." I sat with the comment and realized that "sitting with" means I'm holding something and seeking clarity. In contrast, walking with tends to encompass the bigger questions, where I'm not sure clarity will ever come.

Sitting With

My years of time sitting in the mornings may reflect why the language of "sitting with" comes so easily for me. It's taking a decision, a situation, my own condition, or a message into prayer and seeing what Light comes. There are numerous examples from my journals through the years:

Decisions

Sitting with the question of is it time to resign from Faith & Practice. I don't feel I can say yes to my own call to ministry and continue on the committee. There is joy that I have worked hard and learned much on the committee. But it feels like I'm ready to let go. (Journal, Summer 2005)

My Own Condition

Sitting with my arrogance and judgments, and the knowledge that they grow out of deep fears of not being good enough, and I'm going to prove I'm good enough by always measuring and comparing. (Journal, Fall 2003)

Yesterday I spent some time sitting with the Experiments with Light [see glossary] process, asking the Light to show me what is happen-

---

1 The Friends General Conference Gathering is an annual week-long conference where hundreds of Quakers come together for workshops, worship and celebration (https://www.fgcquaker.org/connect/gathering). Powell House is a Quaker conference center of New York Yearly Meeting in Old Chatham, New York (http://powellhouse.org/).

ing in my life. A very strong sense that I'm running from God — trying to wall out the Spirit. (Journal Summer 2004)

Messages

On Sunday I was sitting with a message of captivity and suffering. We are in our own captivity now, and there is physical suffering and there is suffering of the soul. Our souls are suffering now as we live in bondage to the capitalist system — a system that dehumanizes us, treats us as objects, and urges us to focus only on ourselves. (Journal, November, 2002)

After the close of worship I shared the themes I'd been sitting with — that Quakers are called to find their own voice, each of us, that part of our message is the importance of each voice. Our challenge in corporate worship is to listen with integrity to each voice and struggle to see the whole. Each of us struggles when we find no one else speaking our voice. We struggle with the question of whether we're out of line or too different. And we quiet our own voices. (Journal, Spring 2004)

Walking With

Years ago I heard the story of how Thomas Jefferson ripped out parts of the Bible, seeking where he heard the truth.[2] I couldn't comprehend the certainty involved in such an action. How could one go beyond the truth of the scriptures I'd been taught as a child, to hear where the Living Truth resonates and where it does not? I walked with that question, just wondering what it meant. Walking with questions means I carry them, hold them in my heart and mind, periodically lift them up to the Light, and generally wait for answers or new light. My experience is the answers come. Sometimes I'll find answers in something I read, see or hear, other times answers seem to emerge. It may take years, or even decades, but many of the questions I have walked with have been answered. I trust the Quaker process of deep listening. The following are from my journals:

For years I've been walking with, and holding the question of what does the kingdom of heaven look like today, and I've come to realize

2 More information about Thomas Jefferson's Bible on the Smithsonian's website: http://www.smithsonianmag.com/arts-culture/how-thomas-jefferson-created-his-own-bible-5659505/ (accessed 10/26/2017).

that I hunger for the day when humans live as part of the natural world. (Journal, November 2010)

What is our compelling vision of the world we want? . . . I am walking with what the world would look like if humans lived as part of the natural world. Can we walk back in to the Garden of Eden we left so long ago? (Journal, February 2011)

Quakerism is a tradition that promises answers to life's persistent questions. While many early Quakers started as seekers, the foundation of what we call Quakerism was George Fox's discovery that "there was one, even Christ Jesus, that could speak to thy condition." He found a process that could give him answers. And when he shared that process with others, they could replicate his success. I, too, have walked with questions — what does God's safety look like, what does the kingdom of heaven that is now here look like today, what is today's slavery, and the one I'm walking with right now, what is the tree of knowledge of good and evil in Genesis. These questions represent years of walking with and holding them. (Journal, March 2011, Monadnock Monthly Meeting)

As I hold the questions of how to move forward and listen for the truths my body recognizes, one clear recognition is of the seeds of war embedded in the way I live. I am walking with the question of how to structure my life to decrease the seeds of war. What do I think the seeds of war are, and how am I called to address the seeds of war that I find in my life? I also find myself compelled to hold the broader question of what our society and culture will look like when the seeds of war are no longer embedded in everyday life.

Finding Clarity

Terry Tempest Williams told a high school graduating class that they would find no truths in the world that they did not already know in their bones.[3] When I read that phrase for the first time my body recognized the truth, and I hold it dearly. As I listen for how to move forward in my life, I hold to what I know, ask my questions, and wait for physical recognition of truth before moving forward. For me, there are a range of physical and cognitive signals that might include tears, sweating, a pounding heart or mental clarity.

3 Terry Tempest Williams, Baccalaureate Address, Wasatch Academy, Mt. Pleasant, Utah, May 30, 1999.

At the Emerging Ministries retreat in 2000, representatives from New England Yearly Meeting Ministry and Counsel (M&C) shared information about an upcoming nine-month long spiritual formation program. I sat with the question of whether to participate, and what came with a resounding mental clarity was that I needed to instead commit to a year of monthly personal retreats. Clarity was so strong that when a representative from New England Yearly Meeting M&C asked me to reconsider participating in the program I was able to sit with it and come back to her to say no. When I met with my support committee and they asked what I was hoping for in the personal retreats, I said a greater awareness of the motion of the Spirit in my body, and a better ability to listen and interpret the motion. I wanted to be more confident of what clarity feels like.

Some years ago, Conservative Friend Bill Taber told me that words of the Spirit can come through a place of emotion, and looking for a person's emotions can be a helpful guide to where the Spirit is working with them. Feeling one's emotions deeply can be an important source of information and energy. I watch my emotions, and often tears, as a signal that Spirit is moving through that place and the words I'm speaking. This continues to be an important signal, as I noted in a recent support committee report (see box).

> Yesterday at the M&C meeting I had the committee start by sharing in groups of three around the question of what promptings of the spirit have I followed, which have I avoided. I shared my concerns about whether I've "dropped" my spiritual practice over the last year, as I have struggled to sit outside instead of inside and have not been able to sit still for the hour I'm used to. I found myself moved to tears with a clarity that I have not dropped my practice, but am honestly struggling to learn a different language as I sit outside. That I am able inside to metaphorically speaking sink into the flow, and need to learn to do it outside also. I am so incredibly grateful for that affirmation! (May 2017, Support Committee report)

Another physical sign for me can be dripping sweat in my armpits that is not associated with physical exertion. I first noticed this while serving on New England Yearly Meeting Faith and Practice, where I would leave a day long committee meeting smelling strongly of sweat. I've felt this most often in deep one on one or small group sharing, where I've been given words that speak to someone's condition, either my own or another's.

Being moved to speak is another combination of physical sensations, on a continuum of a very gentle throbbing in my gut to heart pounding and mental clarity. My experience of being called to ministry was a powerful experience of being moved to speak, which included loss of peripheral vision for a short period of time, a pounding heart, and a churning in my gut that made it impossible to eat for a couple of hours. Other times the experience of being moved to speak has been a steady pounding of my heart. I remember one time I was clear to stand without knowing what the message would be, and I'm grateful both that I could be faithful and that the message came while I was standing!

Conclusion

These are my experiences, how I experience the living and vital Spirit. Some of these signals are similar to what I've heard other Friends describe. I make no claim or suggestion that they are universal. Rather, I encourage you to listen yourself, and to pay attention to the signs and signals in your life of the living God at work.

Queries

When have you experienced a deep clarity? What did it feel like?

What physical signs of the Spirit's presence have you experienced?

CHAPTER 4

A Listening Year

Boxed text in this chapter was transcribed from memory of vocal ministry that came through the author in worship.

I NEEDED SOME SPACE. Being responsible for everything while my husband John was in the hospital for three weeks had drained me. But how to get away? I called Brian, a friend who worked as a pastoral counselor at the local hospital. He suggested two nearby retreat centers. Wisdom House had space the following weekend, and Mercy Center had an opening a month later. I reserved both. For the next ten days I anticipated the weekend at Wisdom House. My sons Rainer (five years) and Cameron Jack (three years) listened as I told them I was going away for three days, and John assured me he was recovered enough to care for the boys.

July 2000: Wisdom House

Appointments in Hartford consumed the Friday hours, until around 4 PM when I headed west on Route 44 towards Litchfield. The beautiful afternoon sun with scattered clouds was still high enough that it wasn't directly in my eyes, and the shadows of clouds played across the trees. As I pulled into the gravel parking lot, I was amazed at the size of the three-story building, which was an old convent. I found the entrance and made my way to the office, up the metal stairs from the basement to the main floor. I was assigned a room on the second floor and Sister Rosemarie guided me there, up the elevator and down to the end of the hall. The bathroom and showers were down the hall, and I put my bag down on one of the twin beds.

I took clothes and toiletries from my bag, and quickly arranged them in and on the dresser. I put the crayons, drawing pad and my journal on the desk, and realized that I had no pen. My immediate reaction was to get the pen from the car, but then I decided to flow with what happened, and to accept that I wouldn't be writing. Soon it was time for dinner.

I joined a group finishing up a week's silent retreat in the basement dining room, and we shared a silent buffet-style meal of chicken, rice and vegetables. After dinner, I found the door to the chapel and went into the balcony. I sat quietly for a half hour, letting the silence wash over me.

It was still early, so I headed out for a walk, looking for Topsmead State Forest a mile away. The walk to the forest went along back roads, past huge homes that might once have been farms but clearly were no longer. At Topsmead I walked along the paths and sat on the patio of the beautiful old home on the top of the hill that is the center of the donated land, savoring the joy of being alive.

Saturday was more of the same — breakfast, sitting on the sun deck in worship, feeling the sunshine fill me with light, sitting on the balcony in the chapel, and walking at Topsmead. Saturday afternoon while walking, words came — "We are being called to rediscover what it means to tremble with the Spirit." I held the sentence and wondered if I would be moved to speak at New England Yearly Meeting annual sessions two weeks later.

Back at Wisdom House the oil pastels pulled me, and I drew a multicolored egg, sort of like the huge sculpture in the garden at Wisdom House. It was white in the center, then violet, blue, green, yellow, orange, red and black. The rainbow, the chakras, these colors filled me up. I posted the drawing on the wall over my desk when I got home.

When I left on Sunday morning I drove to see Opus 40, a stone quarry turned into a sculpture, and on my way I stopped at Falconridge, a huge folk festival. What fun to be able to just do what I wanted. To let go of being a mom, a wife, a homeowner, a professional, all the different roles that filled my days.

August 2000: Yearly Meeting

Two weeks after going to Wisdom House John, the boys and I went to New England Yearly Meeting annual sessions, the annual gathering of Quakers in New England. While there I realized that I needed a year of personal retreats. I needed to learn to listen to the Spirit. To listen, I needed time alone. Time and space where I wouldn't be responsible for anyone or anything, so I could just listen. I committed to myself and the Spirit that I would do monthly retreats for a year.

We are being called to rediscover what it means to tremble with the Spirit. The Spirit calls us, and we hesitate. We fear what we might lose should we follow the Spirit — the respect of others, family, money, security. People have been asked to give up each of these in the past to follow the Spirit. And yet when we face the fear of loss we find that there is a place where we are held safely that is always there when nothing else remains. And resting in that place we find ourselves renewed in the Spirit. (New England Yearly Meeting, Bryant College, Rhode Island, August 6, 2000)

August 2000: Mercy Center

When I called in July to schedule a retreat in the solitude space, the sister said there was only one night before October. But upon looking she found two nights, and half of another day. I was able to get parts of three days. Mercy Center is large, with spreading connected buildings. When I arrived in the late afternoon there was a note at the main door, directing me to the solitude space, and I made my way through the corridors and up the stairs to the tower. It had a couch, single bed, table, half bath, and windows on all four sides. One side overlooked Long Island Sound.

> Grey clouds make the decision to go without a clock today disorienting. Sun in early afternoon gave me warmth to go swimming. But now I sit, still drowsy from a nap, wondering what I should do. Draw? Quilt? Walk? Or just sit. And if I were to sit, do I choose a bench by the Sound, a chair on the balcony, or an inside chair? (Journal, Aug 2000)

I struggled. All alone there was no one else to impose structure on my time. I had chosen to fast, and not bring books, so there were no meal times to orient me or books to lose myself in. I was anxious about what I should be doing, and how to best use my time. There weren't any convenient long walks, so I sat and watched the rising tide hide some rocks in the bay, and then the ebbing tide reveal them once again.

I reflected on Edwin Friedman's *A Failure of Nerve: Leadership in the Age of the Quick Fix*, which I had been reading. He talks about three principles of leadership: (1) self-differentiation or becoming who you are meant to be; (2) maintaining a non-anxious presence or not letting yourself be forced to respond by the anxiety of others; and (3) remaining connected to others.

> What Friedman doesn't discuss is that the leader's vision has to be selfless. The vision has to be greater than the leader presenting the vision. In addition, self-differentiation is about the ability to be clear and to separate yourself from the fruits of your actions. You are not a success or failure because of how something you started turns out. Your personal sense of who you are is more secure and deeper. You will always ask, did I do what I could, and what can be done differently next time? But success or failure right now cannot be judged. How are we to know that something or someone was a failure? We can't see all of the ramifications of any action. (Journal, August 2000)

I drove home feeling like not much happened. But I was rested and present. I had my time apart.

September 2000

Mercy Center was the last three days in August, and I would be going to Block Island in mid-October, so I chose not to go away in September. Towards the end of the month I felt like I had no patience with my sons, and realized how much I needed the time away. Time away gave me perspective on the trivial nature of many of the things that irritate and rub in daily life.

October 2000: Block Island Stillness Retreat

Traveling to Block Island, I loved the ferry ride, sitting on the top feeling the sun and the wind. Although it was October and we had been warned to expect rough seas, we had a beautiful Indian summer weekend and the crossing was smooth. Our group gathered at the ferry dock and piled into cars for the ride to the Sprague home site.

We settled into silence after dinner. I worked on the quilt for John and me and then fell asleep. Early Saturday I got up and walked toward the highest point on Block Island. No trespassing signs stopped me on one side, but there was a driveway off the road on the other side also. I walked past the house, and seeing no vehicles, decided to cross the yard to the point behind the house. There was a knoll with a bench, and I sat there, watching the sun come and letting it fill me.

Back at the house I browsed through materials on the coffee table after breakfast. I picked up Henri Nouwen's *The Way of the Heart* from the selections on the table, packed water and a map, and headed for pathways labeled green ways on the map. For the next two hours I walked, read a bit, walked some more, and then read a bit more. Beautiful green trails threaded across the southern part of the island. It was the fall warbler migration and I saw several brilliantly colored small birds flying through the low shrubby trees and brush that edge the trail. As I neared the end of my walk I rationed the book so that I finished it when I was back at the stile crossing the stone wall where I started. The themes of silence, solitude and prayer spoke to me. I was uncomfortable with prayer, because I couldn't forget the formulas I grew up with. However, reading Nouwen, I had the epiphany that for me, singing is also prayer. Sunday morning when I went to the same knoll to wait for the sun, I sang.

Sunday afternoon at home I was irritable with the kids. I continued to be so the rest of the week. After reflection I realized that the downside for me of retreats with groups is that a community is created that I then leave behind. I drew a picture, with the words and music to "Singing Time" (by Rose Fyleman) and "This Pretty Planet" (by Tom Chapin) at the top and bottom, a stone wall with a book resting on the wooden stile, and a figure kneeling at a bench on a knoll looking over the bay with the sun appearing at the horizon. I stuck the picture on the wall above my desk at home.

Vietnam/China, November 11–26, 2000

I traveled to China and Vietnam for two weeks in November 2000, to do some follow-up from my dissertation research in Vietnam and to work with a colleague in China.

This will be my time away for November. I'm grateful for the travel time alone. As I sit on the plane I'm really grateful for not having to attend to anyone else's needs. As a friend said last summer, I was rebelling at being needed. The travel time will be my monthly retreat time. Time to sit back and imagine that I'm the sun, and then to visualize the different planets. Time to look at the full moon and to imagine mentally the trip I'm taking around the globe, literally running away from the sun. We're just over an hour out of Hong Kong now, and I got on the plane in Hartford 23 hours ago. When I got on in Hartford the sun was setting, and then we flew west. As the earth has rotated eastward, we have flown at 500 mph westward. When I see the sun rise in Hong Kong it will have been a 24 hour night.

I brought Rainer's quilt with me to work on, and I think there are elements of showing off to working on a quilt in public. And yet I was interested in having something to do other than reading. I haven't read much at all on this flight. I've worked on Rainer's quilt, slept, ate, meditated, sang to myself, and worked on a story.

I'm singing two songs — a verse from "O Holy City Seen of John," and a verse from "Once to Every Time and Nation." "Give us o Lord the strength to build, the city that has stood too long a dream where laws are love and ways are servanthood. And where the sun doth brightly shine God's grace on human good." And "Though the cause of evil prosper, yet 'tis truth alone be strong. Though her portion be a scaffold and upon the throne be wrong. Yet that scaffold sways the future and behind the dim unknown standeth God within the shadows keeping watch over her own." (Journal entries, November 2000)

While in China I looked for a gift for John. I finally settled on a beautiful scroll painting of bamboo, remembering a story I read once about Bamboo, giving herself as a vessel to carry water to the garden.

In a garden dwelt Bamboo, the most beautiful and beloved dweller of the garden. One day the Gardener came and said "Bamboo, I would use you. But first I must take you and cut you down." Bamboo trembled, slowly bent her glorious head, and said "If you cannot use me unless you cut me down, then do your will and cut." "Bamboo, I would cut your leaves and branches from you, and divide you in two and cut out your heart." She trembled again, and quietly said "Cut and divide." And so the Gardener cut her open, and lay one end of the broken Bamboo in a spring of water, and the other in the field, and the sparkling spring flowed through her to the plants. In that day was Bamboo, once so glorious in her stately beauty, yet more glorious in her brokenness and humility. For in her beauty she was life abundant, but in her brokenness she became a channel of abundant life to the whole world. (Hartford Friends Meeting, November 26, 2000)[1]

1 Anne Hope and Sally Timmel, *Training for Transformation*, Vol 1 (Zimbabwe: Mambo Press, 1984), pp. 153–54.

December 2000: Abbey of Regina Laudis

We stopped by the Abbey in August, when I saw a road sign pointing toward it. The porteress told me to write the Guest Mistress, and I scheduled a stay in December. There was an ice storm the night before, and when I woke up and saw the ice-covered trees, I worried about the roads. But by 10 AM, when I had planned to leave the house, the roads looked okay. I headed to Bethlehem, Connecticut. It's only a twenty-minute drive in good weather, but I drove slowly. The ice coated trees were still, and the overcast sky lent a hushed feeling to the air as I pulled into the Abbey drive.

> I'm somewhat intimidated by the unfamiliarity — fears of doing the wrong thing, disturbing something, breaking the written or unwritten rules. I started by going to the wrong door, not knowing where the guest house was. I parked the car near the Abbey and carried my bag, water bottle and quilt-stuffed pillowcase to the main entrance, where two women, one in habit, one not, were caring for the plants in the foyer. I said that I was coming to stay, and they told me to go inside and ring the bell and wait for someone to come. I did, and after a bit an older woman came and brusquely directed me back to my car, back to the main road, and up to the next driveway, where St. Gregory's, the guesthouse is. She also told me they would expect me at noon in the refectory. (Journal, Dec 2000)

There were cloistered Benedictine nuns, in full habit, chanting Latin prayers six times a day. I went to most of the prayers, and struggled with how to spend my time. After noon prayers and lunch, I spoke with the porteress who offered to have the guest mistress call me. Later that afternoon, Mother Placid did call me. I went up to the refectory to meet with her, and we spoke for almost an hour. The conversation was interrupted periodically by telephone calls, since Mother Placid was on telephone duty. She told stories, and we talked about accepting the Spirit. I was reminded of a phrase from Henri Nouwen's *Our Greatest Gift*, that "the worst thing the flyer can do is to try to catch the catcher. . . . A flyer must fly, and a catcher must catch, and the flyer must trust, with outstretched arms, that his catcher will be there for him."[2] We are like the flyers on a trapeze,

---

2 Henri J. M. Nouwen, *Our Greatest Gift: A Meditation on Dying and Caring* (San Francisco: HarperOne, 1994), p. 67.

trying to grab the person who will catch us. Instead we must let go, and let the Spirit catch us. It's not extended hours praying or meditating that help us connect with the Divine, it's a combination of grace and a readiness to be caught. I walked, listened to the Latin prayers, helped clean, and visited with a couple of other guests. I loved the sense of peace.

January 2001: Young Friends Midwinter

I was at a youth hostel with seventy teenagers for four days — could I make this a *retreat*? Each morning I got up around 6 AM and walked for a half hour or so up the road and onto the trails behind the Friendly Crossways Youth Hostel. Saturday morning the sunrise was divine. Purples, reds and orange filled the horizon as I sat on a snow-covered log on the hillside. The rest of Saturday was filled with activities, cooperative games, and conversations with youth and other adults.

Sunday morning I woke up before dawn with my heart pounding and tears in my eyes, wondering if I would be moved to speak in meeting. I went for a walk and prayed, *Let what needs to be said come forth, and if I need to be the one to speak, let me be ready.* I went farther on my walk than on Saturday and ended up getting lost. The trail came back eventually to the main road, and I realized I had circled the youth hostel.

Sunday we played freeze tag in the snow, and filled the time with laughter and play, in addition to a challenging business session. Monday morning I walked again, and big snowflakes started to come down just as I returned to the youth hostel. We packed and cleaned up quickly, and then headed home.

We are called to look deep inside ourselves to decide what we should be doing. We need to let go of the world's standards of success and failure. Our standards of success and failure have to come from a centered place inside ourselves. The standards the world uses are not true. (Friendly Crossways, January 14, 2001)

February 2001: Woolman Hill

While it's hard to have a retreat when you're in charge, leading the weekend program on "Feeding our Bodies and Souls" was definitely a rest. Driving up to Woolman Hill I saw an exhilarating eighteen red-tailed hawks, perched at different places along the freeway. Heading up the steep drive to Woolman Hill the rest of the world fell away, and I was present. We cooked simple foods and shared food stories. Saturday morning we tried to list all the foods included in our breakfast and where they had come from. A meal of muffins, fruit, oatmeal and coffee had come from all over the world.

We talked of eating, and the power of mindfulness in eating. We considered the invisibility of the hands that have touched our food on the way to us, and wondered about those people. Are they fed? Do they hold our food angrily, roughly, tenderly, sadly, with love? How do those hands, and the hands of those that prepare our food, affect us? Does food that is lovingly grown and prepared contain some invisible energy that makes it more nourishing? It was a present, un-self-conscious time of responding and being, and a chance to renew friendships and make new ones.

> There is a Silence that is greater than the quiet. A Silence that fills our hearts and roots us. We cannot change the world unless we act out of that Silence. It is that Silence that fills and moves us in tune with the Divine. (Woolman Hill, February 4, 2001)

March 2001: Abbey of Regina Laudis

It was a joy to be back with a familiar routine. I put my clothes and things away and then went to prayers and lunch. I worked on a quilt, read a book about animal tracks, and then went to more prayers. Each morning before Mass I took a long walk, and each evening after the last prayers I did yoga in my room.

As I walked up the hill in the woods to the main church the second day, I recognized wildcat tracks in the new snow. I checked them in a reference book later, and confirmed they were indeed wildcat. It was perfect snow for tracking, with a hard crust underneath and an inch of new snow on top.

The church was light-filled, with double rows of clear windows lining both sides of the sanctuary. The metal grille between the sisters and the rest of us was a reminder of their choice to separate themselves. Quakers used to wear plain dress to separate themselves, and I remember reading that some Muslim girls find that wearing a hijab or chador may free them to be more themselves.

How do we each find ways to separate ourselves from the busyness of the world? We have to make some decisions about habitual activities so that minutiae doesn't fill all of our time. How do we separate ourselves enough to create space to focus on deeper things?

April 2001: Falmouth, Massachusetts

John and I were participating in a couples retreat, and all of us were attending a family weekend at Woolman Hill in April, so I didn't schedule a separate weekend for myself. However, I did have a committee meeting in Falmouth, Massachusetts, and I drove over the night before with a friend. A friend in our meeting had a family home near the beach, and she offered to let us stay there overnight.

Saturday morning I headed out into the drizzle and mist around 5:30 AM. Once I got to the beach I walked along the sand. I tried to slow my walk down so that I was walking with the loose sand, sinking in with each step. I finally headed off into a nature area near the shore, wandering in wide pathways with overhanging trees. I sat on a bench beside a pond for awhile, watching two ducks bob gently on the water. As the mist started to rise I realized it was getting late and I'd better get back. I walked until I found a road, and realized I didn't know where I was. I kept walking and soon found a street I recognized.

At the committee meeting there was a selection of books from the Friends General Conference bookstore, and I bought two: *Prayer without Ceasing*, by Candida Palmer, and *Let Your Life Speak* by Parker Palmer. I realized it was time for me to think about what prayer is, and to find a way that I could be comfortable praying.

I had been thinking about prayer beads since I made some for a teenager at the Midwinter gathering. But I kept thinking how kitsch and trite they seemed. Finally, at the end of April, I made some. Four big glass beads, separated from each other by three small beads. One set of three black beads for John and the boys, three clear beads for Quaker committee responsibilities, three blue beads for friends and loved ones, and three green beads for the coming day. For each of the big ones I held it in my fingers, and felt the Presence in all things and the Presence in me. With the beads, I found myself praying for the first time in many years. I still go back to these beads periodically, especially when I need something tangible to focus my mind and prayers.

> We are called to listen. Not for where we're comfortable, capable, effective, but for where the Spirit needs us. When we stay where we're comfortable we don't get stretched and we don't grow. And we believe we did it all by ourselves. (New England Yearly Meeting Committee Day, West Falmouth, MA, April 21, 2001)

Appalachian Trail, May 10–11, 2001

I realized in December that the end of my year of retreats would be a solo backpacking trip, preferably in May. Thursday-Friday worked best, because then the boys could just go to the babysitter.

> I didn't eat breakfast before starting on Thursday, and chose to fast until lunch time on Friday. It wasn't an easy hike, with lots of steep uphill sections, some up rock ledges. When I started getting really stiff I would hold my beads in my shorts pocket and pray — "Guide my feet, lift my feet." Thursday night when I stopped to camp I was very stiff and sore. I spent a lot of time that evening meditating and doing Reiki, thinking about the Chi and sending it to my shoulders and hips. (Journal, May 2001)

As I set up my camp, I started by walking a boundary around it, and saying a prayer for protection as I walked. I put up the tent, but chose to sleep outside where I could watch the stars and be a part of the semi-wild world around me. I listened to a woodpecker, and finally caught a glimpse of a red-crested bird pecking at trees around my camp. I took out the medicinal plants book and looked up some of the wildflowers I'd seen. The most spectacular was a purple trillium. I listened to the sounds change as dusk gave way to night and the birds went to sleep. The insects continued buzzing for quite awhile, but eventually I, too, went to sleep. Several times during the night I woke up. Each time I felt only joy, and after checking out where the almost full moon was in the sky, and the night sounds of the forest, I lay back down and slept.

Thoughts on the trail: We underestimate ourselves and what we can do with a higher power. Sometimes we need to push ourselves physically to let the Presence break through. We can't spend too much time looking way out in front, trying to see the mountain top we work towards. We have to keep our eyes and mind present on the trail where we are.

War is based on the philosophy that the end justifies the means. The end NEVER justifies the means. We can never know all the other strands we don't see working together that may change an end we see as inevitable. We can never know the ends that we create, because we never know all the lives and actions affected. All we can know is the means. Do the means speak of wholeness and love? Since we can never know the end, we need the faith to leave those ends to a higher power, and to focus on whether our lives speak of wholeness and love. Faith is accepting that the ends are not our responsibility. (Hartford Monthly Meeting, May 27, 2001)

Reflections

The year of listening for the Divine Presence helped me to recognize that it's always with us. And maybe my ears and heart were somewhat better trained to listen. The next stage on my journey after the personal retreats would be listening to others and hearing the Divine in them. I knew it was time for me to learn to listen better, especially to John and the boys. I realized I needed to internalize that the process is more important than the outcome, and the end never justifies the means. The end of having a nice garden does not justify excluding my son Cameron Jack (four years old) from the planting. We painted, Cameron Jack and I, and I trusted that the walls would look okay when we were finished.

Queries

What pulls of your daily life could you set aside for a day or week-end to find your own center?

What opportunities for spiritual refreshment do you have in your life?

CHAPTER 5

From Mormon to Quaker

I AM A QUAKER, but my spiritual roots lie in the Mormon church. As I have made the Quaker tradition my own, I have also sought to hear and understand more deeply the treasures in the Mormon tradition. Honoring those treasures deepens my faith. Many Quakers come from other traditions, and the question of how someone came to Quakerism can lead to deep sharing. When people ask how I came to Quakerism, and hear that I grew up Mormon, they tend to express surprise, and often ask how I made such a large jump. I tell them Quakerism wasn't a large jump from the understanding of Mormonism I was raised with, and I share some stories to explain.

The stories I tell are from the Book of Mormon. The Book of Mormon begins with the story of the prophet Lehi and his family as they leave Jerusalem shortly before it is destroyed (around 600 BC). Lehi has a dream one night which includes an image of an iron rod that runs beside a path that takes people to the tree of life. A fog comes up, and the people on the path that are holding the iron rod make it to the tree of life. The people who let go of the iron rod wander away into the wilderness (1 Nephi 8:5–43). Shortly after the dream, Lehi and his family are wandering in the wilderness, not knowing which way to go. Lehi wakes up one morning to find a golden compass outside his tent. This is a special compass, called a liahona, which works according to the faith and diligence of the people. When the people are following God, one needle points in the direction to travel, and the other points in the direction where they will find food (1 Nephi 16:10–28). When the people are not faithful, the two needles spin at random.

Like Lehi, many of us dream of an iron rod, something to hold on to that will let us walk safely through life. And when we wake up, we find ourselves wandering in the wilderness with no more than an internal compass. We are torn between the vision of an iron rod and the reality of our own wanderings with a compass with needles that sometimes just spin. We continue to dream of the iron rod, and we are drawn to the certainty of the iron rod. Some of us seek to make the dream reality by finding traditions that claim to be the iron rod. Others have let go of the dream to engage fully with the compass in the wilderness. Traditions tending more toward the compass can be very challenging in times when the inner guide seems silent and one is having trouble hearing. Traditions claiming to provide an iron rod can provide clear day-to-day guidance, but must be checked with the compass on a regular basis, lest one end up someplace completely different than desired. Developing in ourselves the fluidity to use each of these approaches at different times may allow us to better nourish our spiritual lives.

Within the Mormon community there are people who follow each of these paths. The images of the people that seek an iron rod and people that seek a liahona were contrasted in an influential 1969 essay by Richard Poll in a liberal Mormon publication.[1] I share these stories to make it clear the Mormon tradition also has a place for people seeking to hear deeply the voice of the Spirit, in addition to holding the more public stereotype of a religion for people who are seeking fixed rules to guide them through life.

I was brought up in a family working to maintain a place within the Mormon tradition for people heeding the compass. I remember coming home from Sunday School as a young teen, after a lesson on a story from the Book of Mormon. The prophet Nephi was told to go back to Jerusalem to get the records of his people (written on gold plates) from a man called Laban. He meets a drunken Laban on the street, and God tells him to kill Laban, dress in his clothes and go get the plates from Laban's house (1 Nephi 4:7–13). After mentioning the topic of the class to my mother, she asked why God had Nephi kill Laban. I parroted the response from my teacher: the plates were very important, and killing Laban was the only way to get them. Mom's response was "Don't you think God could have figured out another way?" Her question has continued to resonate with me. Does what a religion teaches align with my deepest sense of goodness and love? Is the authority the community respects in alignment with my own Guide? These stories, and the questioning and example of my parents

---

1 More information on Richard Poll can be found on Wikipedia's website: http://en.wikipedia.org/wiki/Richard_D._Poll (accessed 10/26/2017).

and siblings, make it difficult for me to denigrate the Mormon church. I have plenty of experience with the human frailties of people in leadership positions in the Mormon church. I also have a wealth of experience of thoughtful seekers within the Mormon church, heeding the guidance of the Spirit of Truth and Love they feel in their hearts and bodies.

I have tried to listen to the values and perspectives of the culture and communities around me with an ear that is also listening for when the values do not feel right. One of the key tensions I carry in my life is between cultural authority and spiritual authority. How does what I hear from the community around me resonate with my own internal compass? I know that we are all, to varying degrees, stuck in a cultural framework. When we experience the Divine, powerful possibilities open up. We look at our world with new eyes and yearn to bring the outer world into alignment with the inner sense of rightness and love. But at every turn we are hampered by how well we can step outside of the cultural norms we grew up with.

The Hebrew scriptures are full of stories of how people understood their interaction with the Divine. And most of those stories are of people deeply embedded in a patriarchal framework and culture, prevalent at the time. Jesus was able to see his culture and the rigid hierarchies of power in a new way. The key threat he posed to the established order of both the Roman and Jewish hierarchies was an alternative vision of how people could live together, based on love and equality. The vision is not easy to grasp, and after the four gospels, the remaining books of the Christian scripture step back partway into the patriarchal culture and the "us vs. them" worldview.

Joseph Smith experienced the Divine Presence. The Mormon tradition, as I believe all religions have, started with an interaction between humans and the Divine. However, many religions have elaborate cultural structures, detracting from the original interaction with the Divine. When I started reading Quaker history, I could immediately see parallels between George Fox and Joseph Smith. Both of them had powerful experiences of the Divine. And on those experiences they each built a structure to create a unique religious community. The structure that Joseph Smith built has many pieces that feel out of alignment to me. The structure is a male hierarchy, with exclusive rewards for Mormons.

Quakerism, in contrast, has a fairly flat structure, with local con-gregations (monthly meetings) arranged into regional (quarterly) and area (yearly meeting) groups. Leadership varies, with some Quaker traditions employing pastors. All Quaker organizations have clerks, who are the volunteer leaders of the congregation, generally serving for two to three year terms. What all Quakers also share is a reliance on a corporate decision-making process of deep communal listening for the Inward Teacher. At its best, every piece of the deci-sion-making process points back to the interaction with the Spirit. I know that it doesn't always work. But I find myself more able to heed the invitation of the Spirit to radical re-visioning of how I live within the Religious Society of Friends rather than within Mormonism.

God is Still Speaking

Joseph Smith, like George Fox, worked to create a religious institu-tion to embody the reality that the heavens are still open. Mormons know God continues to speak to us. Every religion which believes in continuing revelation faces the challenge of how to control for false prophets. The question is, knowing the power of the Spirit, how will the community discern that it is led by the One Spirit, and not by their own wishes, emotions, or the adversary? Another way to approach the question is to ask where the authority is for discerning Truth. Some churches rely on written words such as the Bible or other texts. Other traditions use a hierarchy which vests authority in particular leaders. Quakers put the responsibility in the community listening together. Mormons have placed responsibility in a hierarchy of "General Authorities." Like the explanation of Dostoevsky's *Grand Inquisitor*,[2] the structure of the Mormon church assumes the unwillingness (and inability) of many people to accept responsibility for their own freedom and the need for some kind of spiritual author-ity. Many of us seek an iron rod, a sure path. And the Mormon Church speaks with certainty of the sureness of their path. Within the struc-ture there is one man, the prophet, who is given authority to hear clearly what God speaks to the Church, and specific individuals are designated to hear and understand for those under their guidance

2 Fyodor Dostoevsky, *The Brothers' Karamazov*, translated by Richard Pevear (New York: Farrar, Strauss & Giroux).

within the corporate structure. The hierarchy is embedded within a cultural framework of patriarchy, justified with reference to the scriptures.

Another part of acknowledging how God continues to speak is by emphasizing the study and personal spiritual practice involved in preparing oneself for encounters with the Holy Spirit. Within the Mormon tradition, families and individuals are encouraged to study the scriptures. I remember being awoken early in the morning as a child, before school, so that we could read the scriptures together. Dad took the lead in this endeavor. He would wake up the five oldest girls and gather us on the floor around the wood stove, wrapped in blankets to keep warm. We sat on the floor, sometimes dozing as Dad read. He would stop periodically and ask us questions, maybe so that we'd be more likely to stay awake. We gathered for family prayer before breakfast or bedtime at night. We gathered in a circle, sang a song and then knelt together in prayer, thanking God for our blessings and asking for help in our daily lives. One of the common phrases was to bless the leaders of the church and the leaders of the country.

Teenagers in the Mormon Church are expected to attend seminary, a program of study offered either in the morning before school (early morning seminary), during school (released time, offered primarily in Utah and Idaho), or as independent study where the youth are more spread out. The seminary program includes studying the scriptures (the Bible, Book of Mormon, Doctrine & Covenants and Pearl of Great Price), memorizing key passages, and coming to one's own testimony of the truth of the Mormon church and Gospel. There is a powerful emphasis on asking for a personal confirmation of the truth. Joseph Smith's first experience of the Divine grew out of reading James 1:5–6, "If any of you lack wisdom, let him ask of God — who giveth to all men liberally and upbraideth not; and it shall be given him. But let him ask in faith, nothing wavering."[3] And just as Joseph Smith asked, we, too, were encouraged to ask. I felt the warmth of the Spirit in my body when I prayed about the truth of the Book of Mormon.

For Mormons, the first Sunday of each month is called Fast Sunday. Members are encouraged to fast for two or three meals and

---

3 From *The King James Bible*.

to donate the money they would have spent on food, their "fast offering," to the church to use for welfare assistance. In addition to fasting, the service on Fast Sunday is open worship where individuals share messages as they are led, about their own beliefs and how the Spirit is working in their lives. I remember standing during Fast and Testimony meeting to bear my testimony; I knew the church was true, and the Book of Mormon was the word of God.

In addition to daily spiritual practice and weekly church attendance, many young men and women were encouraged to spend eighteen to twenty-four months of their lives, paid for by themselves and their families, teaching people about the Mormon church. The experience of missionary work, of asking the question over and over, "What does the Spirit want me to do?" praying and asking which street to walk down, which doors to knock on, seeking to be completely obedient to the immediate promptings of the Divine, in a community of others with the same goal, is a very powerful formative experience. Time and again individuals will refer to their mission as the best two years of their lives. I waited some months after I turned twenty-one, the age at which young women were encouraged to go on missions, before praying to ask whether I should go. I knew I couldn't ask for guidance until I was willing to accept the answer, and I didn't want to go on a mission. I was relieved to be clear after praying that I didn't need to go. Now, I do my best to practice daily obedience to Divine guidance, but sometimes yearn for the immersive experience of Mormon missionaries, in some other form.

The Kingdom of Heaven on Earth — in the World but Not of the World

The Mormon Church honors the importance of the spiritual community being the center of one's focus. Being Mormon was at the center of my world for the first twenty-something years of my life. As a family we read the scriptures, we tried to have Family Home Evening a couple of times a month, and we went to church for three hours every Sunday. But being Mormon isn't about Sundays — it's about one's entire life. It's about the certainty of one's place in the world, the sense of one's separateness from the world, and the culture that serves to keep members of the church distinct.

While the Mormon church honors the importance of the spiritual community, it fails to grasp Jesus's message that there is no Jew or Gentile, and that we are all a part of the community regardless of whether we have been baptized into the Mormon church. While I was growing up, there was a strong sense of being different from (and better than) the non-Mormons around me. I assumed the non-Mormons didn't know what I knew about one's place in the world. They only had the Bible — they didn't have the Book of Mormon and the other scriptures. And they didn't have temples, so they weren't going to be together as families for eternity, as Mormon families will be who are sealed in the temple. They also didn't have the Word of Wisdom, which is the source of the dietary guidelines and prohibition against alcohol, tobacco and coffee that Mormons follow.

Some of the differences that kept us apart from the world as Mormons were misunderstandings, and some were clearly cultural. Mormon church leaders advise all members to have a year's supply of food stored — this means all the food and water (or water purification system) a family would need to eat for an entire year. Having food storage meant we ate a lot of foods with long shelf lives, such as canned and dried foods. The storage had to be rotated on a regular basis, so the family ate from the food storage and replenished it with new purchases. Years ago, while leading a class exercise on food culture, a Mormon graduate student I worked with shared her experience as a child of asking a friend why her family used real onions when the dried onions were so much less hassle. Her own family always used dried, as they were part of the family food storage. It was an example for her at the time of just another way her family was different.

Every December, my parents and siblings and I went to Tithing Settlement, where we confirmed to the leaders of the congregation that we paid a full 10% of our income to The Church of Jesus Christ of Latter Day Saints (LDS Church, see glossary) as tithing. The law of tithing that Mormons practice assures the financial security of the LDS Church and the Mormon institutions. Brigham Young University (BYU), as a Mormon school, has different Mormon and non-Mormon tuition rates, since it is supported by the tithing of Mormons. The Law of Tithing also assures those who follow it have a sense of abundance — they can live on 10% less than they make. Many stories are told of the blessings, financial and otherwise, which come when people pay their tithing. Unexpected doors open, money shows up, and all which is needed is provided when people pay their tithing. The Law of Tithing also honors the truth that all we have belongs to God.

Another truth held by the LDS Church is the need to care with love for all the members of the community. Within each local congregation there are a number of organizations: the Priesthood for the men, Relief Society for the women, Mutual for the teenagers, Scouts for the boys, and Primary for the kids. These organizations make it possible for leaders to be aware of members of the congregation in both the positive sense of caring for their needs, and in the negative sense of people feeling like they're always being watched and judged. Within the Relief Society, a pair of visiting teachers is assigned to visit and check in with each woman on a monthly basis. Within the Priesthood a pair of home teachers is assigned to visit and check in with each household on a monthly basis. These regular visits can be done as a sincere service, helping to deepen connection and build community. Converts to Mormonism are welcomed into a large global community which helps them as needed. This church community tends to be the focus of the social life of members, limiting for many their activities in the larger world.

My Path to Quakers

When I look back on my college years, the patterns I see in myself are of idealism, impatience and intolerance combined with a yearning for knowledge and growth. At BYU, where I started my college career, I struggled with the tension between my own internal compass and the cultural standards used by those around me. My freshman year, I was devastated to find most other students weren't as interested as I was in going to lectures and seminars just to learn. I saw college as an opportunity to learn and know my place in the world, to get an education in the richest sense of the word. I had been isolated in high school in a small Idaho town, and while in college, I was thrilled to have friends and interesting talks to go to, foreign movies to see, and a universe of other extra-curricular learning opportunities. However, my grades showed my lack of focus on my classes. After two years I lost my scholarship because of low grades. While home in Idaho the following summer, I started looking for other schools to attend. I was thumbing through Peterson's Guide in May or June, in search of schools whose application deadline had not yet passed, when I found St. John's College in Santa Fe, New Mexico. St. John's College has only one course of study, focused on reading great books and discussing them together, and the vision was very appealing. At BYU I had always sought people to discuss whatever I was reading. I applied to St. John's College, and was accepted.

At St. John's College I had my first opportunity to live within a non-Mormon environment. Yes, I'd had some experience in grade school and high school, but going to St. John's was different. I was the only Mormon in an environment that had no respect and little tolerance for a life of faith in anything except logic and science. The local Mormon community was equally wary of me — the Bishop's (see glossary) daughter told me her father said Mormons couldn't go to St. John's College, because it was against their religion. Still, I tried to see with the eyes of my fellow non-Mormon students. There was exhilaration as we talked and reflected and shared, and loneliness as I sought to be heard and understood. As a nineteen-year-old I became ashamed of my faith, seeing it for the first time with the eyes of the liberal intellectual. My own yearning to be accepted and understood made it difficult for me to be so far outside of the norms of the community at St. John's. It was too hard for me to defend myself to the skeptical intellectuals. I couldn't answer their questions from a place of reason, and I wasn't ready to speak to them from the Spirit. I only stayed at St. John's for one year before going back to BYU. But once back at there I couldn't fit in either, and I left for the University of Washington. In Seattle I found friends and built a community of primarily Mormon friends who shared and played together, while leading a separate school life where I studied philosophy.

Leaving the Mormon church was an extended process for me. At the beginning of my movement out of the Mormon church, while at St. John's College, I had a good friend tell me that I wouldn't be able to fully leave until I wasn't angry. He helped me understand that as long as I was angry at the Mormon church, I would still be reacting to it in my life. I took another three to four years of varying degrees of activity before I was really ready to leave the church. Several threads led me out of the Mormon church. The greatest frustration was always having to struggle to make the church big enough to include me. I knew that the foundational Truth had room for reflection, criticism and deep listening. But the implementation of the doctrine in the community of the living Mormon church was threatened by alternative voices. I was tired of putting so much of my spiritual energy into asking my community to be open to questioning and reflection. There was little room in the Church for discussing patriarchy, hierarchy, equality and what it would mean to build a loving community of equals. The spiritual and cultural center of gravity in the body of the Mormon church was too different from my own, and I wanted the space in my life to not be continually defensive.

I didn't take the final step of asking my name be removed from the records of the Mormon church until after I met my husband John (who was raised Southern Baptist) and we committed to finding a belief system we could share. When I left the Mormon church I wrote a formal letter asking my name be removed from the records of the church. My family was hurt. There were mixed reactions from my siblings and mother. My youngest sister, eight years old at the time, wanted to know why I didn't want to be part of their forever family. Another sister was somewhat more supportive and said there were some things we would just have to leave up to God to straighten out. But despite their initial anger and disappointment at my decision, I have maintained strong ties with my family. Some of my siblings have also left the Mormon church; others remain quite active Mormons.

As a child I had read a couple of novels about Quakers that I really enjoyed — I Take Thee, Serenity, by Daisy Newman, and They Loved to Laugh, by Kathryn Worth. When John and I moved to Cairo, Egypt in August of 1990, I was pleased to find there was a Quaker worship group. Shortly after we arrived in Cairo we called and started to attend. It was there, during the first Gulf War, that I found people who felt as I did about the complexity of the situation and the short-sightedness of the international response. After a year attending the worship group in Cairo, Egypt, we returned to the United States and moved to Ithaca, New York for graduate school. The first semester we were there we went to meeting for worship when we didn't have too much studying to do. But the next year we made a concerted effort to participate and to attend on a regular basis. We started going to business meeting and to committee meetings. And as we began to participate in Quaker process, I realized how much I appreciated the structures of the Religious Society of Friends. The following year we moved to Vietnam and spent sixteen months in Hanoi. There we met informally with a handful of other Quakers. I missed meeting for business, and the opportunities for coming to know others in their humanness, which is most apparent as we try to take action and make decisions together. When we came back to Ithaca, I applied for membership to my local meeting.

My Sense of Community

One of the threads in my life is my yearning to belong, to fit in, and my own willingness to bend in order to fit. My yearning is in constant tension with the desire for freedom and clarity of vision that comes from standing on the edge. As a child my family was on the edge of the Mormon church. My parents were very active, but their questioning, thoughtful approach to the teachings of the Mormon church was not widely understood. As a teenager I was on the edge in my high school. There my interest in learning, as a girl in a rural farming community, kept me on the fringes. When I started college at BYU, the community was large enough that I could find others who were close to where I was. But again, my desire to question authority and to learn and understand a breadth of subjects, as well as the loss of my full tuition scholarship, brought me to the fringes.

At St. John's College I was on the edges in part because of my faith history. But even as I let go of my faith, I was still on the edge. When I moved to Seattle, I worked for a time and found myself much more within a community of other Mormon young adults. We played and worshiped together, and relaxed and had fun.

These questions of what community is, what it means, how we create and build it together are a key part of my life. And yet the desire for community is balanced with my yearning for the clarity of the edges. I still find myself called to the edges — I've held a part-time academic position since finishing graduate school, and have treasured the independence and flexibility of not being judged by the tenure metric. I also value the time I have to read and reflect on a broad canvas as a part-time faculty member. In the different parts of my life

I continue to balance the yearning for a "home" community and the hunger for the space in which to hear and see more clearly how the Spirit calls.

Queries

What faith tradition were you raised in? How does that tradition continue to shape you?

What faith traditions have you left? What new traditions have you embraced?

SECTION 2

*What Canst
Thou Say*

Margaret Fell remembered the challenge George Fox issues the first time she heard him preach: "You will say Christ saith this, and the apostles say this; but what canst thou say? Art thou a child of Light and hast walked in the Light, and what thou speakest is it inwardly from God?"[1]

The essays in this section are grounded in my spiritual journey, and are my response to the challenge George Fox issued. I have sought to walk in the Light, and what I share below is inwardly from that Divine Source. The essays are organized in approximately chronological order of when a solid version of the ideas in a given essay was first completed.

1 From "The testimony of Margaret Fox concerning her late husband," in George Fox, *Journal*, 1694, p. ii; bicentenial edition, 1891, vol 2, pp. 512–14, quoted in *Quaker Faith and Practice*, 2nd ed. (London: Yearly Meeting of the Religious Society of Friends [Quakers] in Britain), #19:07.

CHAPTER 6

Our Hope for a New Life

This essay was published in Quaker Life *(May–June 2008). I was preparing to give a sermon at a Quaker church in Massachusetts, and I was led to preach on 1 Corinthians 15: 12–19 on the resurrection. The Epistles to the Corinthians from Paul are one side of a correspondence. This essay is one way the other side of that conversation might have gone, as an imaginary epistle from the Ministry and Counsel committee of the church at Corinth to the apostle Paul, following the receipt of what we now call the First Epistle to the Corinthians.*

To our beloved Paul, called to be an apostle. Grace to you and peace from God our Father and the Lord Jesus Christ. We send this message to you with gratitude for the love you have shown us. You came to us and brought God's message of hope, the message of Christ Jesus that invites us to enter into the kingdom of God. We lived in the world, as part of the world, knowing not the reality of God's world. Your teaching has brought us to be infants in Christ.

You taught us of gifts from the Spirit. Through the people in our community, we see your teachings of these gifts. There are those with gifts of wisdom, whose insights open our understanding. There are those with gifts of teaching, whose lessons we try to live. There are those with gifts of music, where we hear the eternal in their songs. There are those with gifts of generosity of heart, where we feel God's love through their actions. There are those who care for our children where we watch our children come to feel God's love. There are those who care for our building, whose work supports and holds our community together. We see so many gifts among us, reminding us that all of these gifts come from the same Spirit. We see that there is much work to be done in building God's kingdom here on Earth, and it requires many different gifts. And we have each been given some of those necessary gifts. You caution us about eyeing the gifts of another, and lusting after those gifts in our hearts. You tell us that all of our gifts are needed. We give thanks for your teaching.

You also taught us of love, telling us that the most precious spiritual gift we should aspire to is love. That without it we are nothing. That whatever work we do in this world, however beautiful our music, our art, our writing, our teaching, our food, that if we do it without love, we are but a clashing cymbal. That if we give shelter to the poor, food to the hungry, care for the sick, give away everything we own to the poor, but do not have love, we have gained nothing. We give thanks for your teaching.

We cannot describe all the ways our lives have changed because of your work among us, as you shared with us the power of the Spirit as it calls us to be more wholly God's people. Before your journey we did not know that every day the Spirit invites each one of us to listen, to come to know the Spirit at the center of the universe that holds each one of us. And through your preaching you have brought many to that center. We give thanks for your teaching.

But we must also speak plainly, and seek to settle our disagreements with you directly, as you have taught us. Parts of your most recent epistle have led to dissension among us. As ministry and counsel we have struggled with your message, and with how best to help our community understand that message. In your letter you remind us that when you came to us you came in weakness and fear and much trembling, and your message and proclamation were not with persuasive words of wisdom, but with a demonstration of spirit and power. And we heard and recognized the spiritual power in your message. That power is what brought us together with you in Christ.

In your writings to us on the resurrection you give us subtle arguments: You say if there is no resurrection, then Christ cannot be raised. This is true. If there is no resurrection then no one is raised from the dead. And if there is no resurrection, those who have said that God raised Christ from the dead have lied. That is also true. And then you go on — If Christ has not been raised, then empty is your teaching and our faith, and our faith is in vain, and we are still in our sins, and those who have fallen asleep in Christ have perished. We so value and trust your guidance that we hesitate to speak. But we struggle to understand this message.

Within our community there are many different understandings of this resurrection from the dead. Some of us say there is no resurrection after death, that when we die that is the end. And they say that the stories of the sayings of Jesus speak to a new life now. That we can live as Christians, believing in the teachings of this Jesus, without saying there is a resurrection after death.

Others say there is a resurrection only of the just, and for the unjust, death is the end. They say that when we die, those whose works of righteousness outweigh their sins will rise again into eternal life with God. They believe that the teachings of Jesus call us to works of righteousness, so that we may come into eternal life in the company of saints when we die.

Still others say there is a resurrection for all. That God's love for each of us, as demonstrated in the love his son, Jesus Christ, has shown us, could not rest with anything other than the resurrection of all.

Among those who say there will be a resurrection, some say it will be of spirit, and some say it will be a resurrection of flesh. For those who believe in a resurrection of spirit, they believe that our spirits will continue to exist in some manner after we die. For those who say it will be a resurrection in the flesh, they believe that our bodies and spirits will be reunited after we die, and our bodies will be renewed into an eternal flesh.

There are many beliefs: There will be a resurrection. There will not be a resurrection. There will be a resurrection for some. There will be a resurrection for all. There will be a resurrection in the Spirit. There will be a resurrection in the flesh. These are very real differences and when we come together to convince each other of the truth of our own beliefs about the resurrection, it leads only to dissension and argument.

But when we sit together and listen for the wisdom and power in your message and in the living Spirit that guides us, we know that how the living Christ has come to be is a mystery. Whether it is by resurrection of the Spirit, resurrection in the flesh, or some other way, we do not know. Perhaps as infants in Christ we are not ready to understand the mysteries that you write of.

We also know that even if Christ has not been raised, the teachings and path of Jesus called Christ, shown to us by you and other teachers, are not empty. Your teaching is not empty, our faith is not empty, and our faith is not in vain. We speak of that power that brings us to new life every day, as we heed the promptings of the Spirit.

What we believe and share together is an awareness of how our lives have been made new through your ministry. We have been taken from our lives as natural men and women and shown a new vision of the world. We are come into a world where love is the first movement in our hearts to our brothers and sisters.

There was a man, a shopkeeper, who worked each day seeking to get the greatest advantage for himself in every sale or purchase that he made. He worried that he would not have enough to care for himself in his old age. His days were full of arguments, anger and jealousy as he worked to be sure that whatever happened, he came out ahead. And then one day a child came to his shop, a child who shared her story of need with such gentleness, hope and love that the shopkeeper's heart was touched. His eyes were opened to the emptiness in his own life. And his heart was moved and his life changed. So, also, are our lives changed when we are touched by the love and grace of God.

You say that if our hope in Christ is only for this life, then we are a most pitiable people. And yet we find that our hope in Christ is realized in this life, when we find our lives made new, through the gentle workings of the Spirit in our hearts. Our hearts are touched, not through the arguments, but by the transforming power of love and of the living Christ.

We testify to you of how our lives have changed. Each one of us has stories to tell of being angry and bitter but transforming our reactions into love. We have stories of how once we would have argued, and now we can listen humbly and hear the good in the hearts of those with whom we disagree. We know that their hearts are human and frail as our own, and they too can be brought to rise again through the Spirit that calls us all. We have stories to tell of the forgiveness that we find in our hearts for those who have harmed us, of the love that we feel through the power of the Spirit that you led us into.

We know that we are yet infants in Christ. That every day we fail to live up to your teachings. And every day we fall short in living what we have heard of the teachings of Jesus. And yet every day we try again, resolved anew with each daybreak, to hold in our hearts the love and life shown to us by the power of the Spirit. And we hold tightly to our hope that our lives will continue to be made new, through the transforming power of the living God.

May the grace of the Lord Jesus be with you. Our love to you in Christ Jesus.

Query

When have you experienced new openings to truth that changed your previous understanding and judgments?

CHAPTER 7

On Being Grafted Into the Root

An earlier version of the following essay was delivered at Beacon Hill Friends House in October 2007 as part of their "Listen!" series. That talk was published as a Beacon Hill pamphlet in the spring of 2008. It is included here in revised form with permission. For this lecture I was drawn to integrate images of grafting from the Book of Mormon, the Bible, and Quaker texts, and to explore my own experience of leaving one faith tradition for another in the context of the parables of grafting.

IF YOU'RE GOING TO GROW OLIVE TREES, there are three main tasks to keep the tree fruitful: regular pruning, digging up and loosening the ground around the trunk and under the branches a couple of times a year, and mixing manure or another fertilizer into the loosened soil. With this kind of care, olive trees can be quite prolific and lead very long lives. New shoots and new roots renew the tree and keep it fruitful for hundreds of years.

Fossilized leaves of the wild predecessors of the domestic olive trees have been dated to 37,000 BC. Olive trees are believed to have first been grafted, replanted, and tamed around 6,000 BC. They were cultivated in Crete and Syria over 5,000 years ago. Mediterranean cultures, including the Middle East, center around the riches of the olive tree. Violence in the West Bank over the past fifty years has often included destruction of Palestinian olive groves. There are stories in Greek and Roman mythology, and in the Bible, of the ritual uses of olive oil.

Olive trees have root balls that continue to grow and send out new shoots and new roots for hundreds of years. Every year these new shoots come up around the main trunk. If the shoots aren't pruned, you get a tree that spreads out and puts too much energy into the wood growth, leading to a poorer quality olive/fruit crop. Old trees need to be pruned extensively to be most fruitful. Even after a thorough spring pruning, new shoots can grow to be waist high by the fall. In my life, I too, send out numerous metaphorical shoots, exploring new things and ideas. I wonder if I would be more fruitful with regular pruning.

Botanists say an olive trunk can live to be around 700 years old, although trees have been dated to as old as 1,600 years. And when the primary trunk eventually dies, it can be cut off and new shoots will grow in its place. This is a wonderful image of the potential for families, communities, religions and other traditions to live on, as new shoots grow or are brought in to sustain the roots, and then new roots grow.

In addition to their capacity for growth, olive trees are also resilient. In his book, *Olives: the Life and Lore of a Noble Fruit*,[1] Mort Rosenblum tells the story of the author Lawrence Durrell, who moved to southern France and bought an olive grove in 1957. This was one year after a winter so severe that many olive trees were killed. January of 1956 had been unseasonably warm, so the sap started flowing. Then in a matter of a few hours the temperature fell to less than 20°F. Trunks froze and exploded. But a year later, when Durrell visited an olive grove, healthy green shoots sprouted from the roots. Within four years, with proper pruning and tending, the shoots would again bear fruit, and the roots could still live for centuries.

Olive trees, with their ancient, twisted trunks, and their silver, grey-green leaves have been the inspiration of painters and authors. They are a symbol of longevity, of fruitfulness, of regeneration and hope. The use of olive trees in the two stories we're going to look at challenges us to remember these characteristics as a background for the stories.

Let's turn now to grafting. Grafting is when you take a portion of one plant, called the bud or scion, and put it with another plant, the understock, so they grow together into one.[2] The primary use of grafting for olive trees is in propagating varieties which don't root easily. In addition, when olive trees are grown from seeds they put down one deep tap root, which means the tree grows more slowly and cannot take full advantage of surface irrigation and fertilizers.

---

1 Mort Rosenblum, *Olives: The Life and Lore of a Noble Fruit* (New York: North Point Press, 1996).

2 Montague Free, *Plant Propagation in Pictures*, revised and edited by Marjorie J. Dietz (Garden City, New York: Doubleday & Co., 1979), p. 202.

Another use of grafting for olive trees is to change the variety of olives being grown and to make the trees more productive.

For grafting to take, the understock and the scion must be related. To review some basic botany, the growing edge of a tree is the cambium layer. On the inside of the cambium layer is the xylem, where the water and minerals are carried. On the outside of the cambium layer is the phloem, where sugar and other products of photosynthesis are carried. Grafting requires that the cambium layer of the understock and the scion be aligned, so that the xylem and the phloem can come together and nutrient flow can come into the scion, thus eventually fusing the two plants into one. After preparing the scion by removing buds and making the appropriately angled cut, the end of the scion is inserted into a similarly angled cut in the understock. The graft is then taped or tied together and held steady until the two plants have grown together.[3]

This background on olive trees will help us better explore two parables of olive trees and grafting, one from the Bible, and one from the Book of Mormon. In Romans chapter 11, Paul uses the metaphor of grafting in a chapter that begins with the question, "Has God rejected his people?" The chapter continues as Paul makes it clear that he considers the Jews and the Jewish tradition to be the source of the nourishing sap that will feed the Gentiles and make them fruitful. And while Paul believes many of the Jews have rejected God's path of righteousness, and have been broken off because of their unbelief, Paul sees their transgression as contributing to the growing life of the Spirit among the Gentiles. Paul hopes the Jews will be stirred to emulate the Gentiles. "For if their rejection [of God] has led to the world coming into friendship or relationship with God, their acceptance [of God] means life from the dead!"[4]

Then we come to the olive tree: "If the root is consecrated, so are the branches."[5] Since the root is the people of Israel, who have been chosen by God and have not been rejected, then the branches are also consecrated. Paul goes on, "But if some of the branches have been lopped off, and you, a wild olive, have been grafted in among them, and have come to share the same root and sap as the olive, do not

3 Free, *Plant Propagation in Pictures*, p. 203.
4 Romans 11:15, author's translation.
5 Romans 11:16, author's translation.

make yourself superior to the branches. If you do so, remember that it is not you who sustain the root, the root sustains you."[6]

Paul appears to say the Romans, the Gentiles to whom he is speaking, have been cut from the wild olive trees where they were growing. Branches from the cultivated tree have been cut off to make a place for them, and they have been grafted in to the cultivated understock of the Jewish tradition. He warns the Roman branches of the wild tree against arrogance, against considering themselves as superior to the original branches. After all, the branches don't sustain the root, the root sustains the branches.

Paul's metaphor is curious, because in the cultivation of olive trees the wild rootstock is where the strength is, and the cultivated branches are where the fruit is. He has reversed these images — in his metaphor, the strength comes from the cultivated rootstock, and the branches of the wild tree are grafted in.

But let's go back to his story — to quote Romans:

> You will say, "branches were lopped off so that I might be grafted in." Very well: they were lopped off for lack of faith, and by faith you hold your place. Put away your pride and be on your guard; for if God did not spare the native branches, no more will he spare you. Observe the kindness and the severity of God — severity to those who fell away, divine kindness to you, if only you remain within its scope. Otherwise you too will be cut off, whereas they, if they do not continue faithless, will be grafted in; for it is in God's power to graft them in again. For if you were cut from your native wild olive and against all nature grafted into the cultivated olive, how much more readily will they, the natural olive branches, be grafted in to their native stock."[7]

We have an image of a tree with branches but no fruits. Branches are then broken off because of unbelief or because of poor fruits, so other branches might be grafted in. The branches brought from elsewhere to feed on the roots, and hopefully to bear fruits, are warned against forgetting those roots are their source; if the new branches are not faithful and fruitful, they too might be cut off, and the original branches brought back. Paul appears to be warning the Romans against complacency, reminding them they too could be cut off if

6 Romans 11:17–18, author's translation.
7 Romans 11:19–24, author's translation.

they fall away from the path. We can take this story as a story of racial and ethnic superiority, with the rootstock being the people of Israel. But we could also seek more potential in this story: What is the rootstock those who come to the truth are grafted into? Paul suggests it is the people of Israel, but we will come back to other possibilities.

I want to share another story about grafting now, which comes from my own religious heritage. The Book of Mormon tells the story of a group of people who leave Jerusalem shortly before it is destroyed because of a dream given to their leader, the prophet Lehi. They travel into the desert, to the edge of the sea. God then teaches them how to build a boat, and they travel to a new world, where they settle. There is an underpinning of the Jewish tradition, and later in the Book of Mormon, Jesus appears to them. Thus Mormonism is a branch of the Judeo-Christian tradition. Mormons recognize four books of scripture: the Bible, the Book of Mormon, the Doctrine & Covenants (which are modern day revelations to Mormon prophets), and the Pearl of Great Price, another story of Abraham. The allegory of the olive tree, told in the book of Jacob, is attributed to Zenos, a prophet from before the time the group left Jerusalem. The story goes as follows: The Lord says he's going to liken Israel to a tame olive tree, nourished in a vineyard among the vines, which then grows old and begins to decay. And the master of the vineyard comes, sees it, prunes it, digs around it, and fertilizes it, hoping it will grow and send out new shoots. After many days it does send out new shoots, but the top of the tree begins to decay.[8]

To paraphrase what the master of the vineyard says to his servant, "It grieves me to lose this tree. Go bring some branches from a wild olive tree. Then we'll cut off the top of this tree, burn the dead and dying branches, and graft in the branches from the wild olive tree, hoping to save the rootstock." The master also decides to cut some of the new shoots from around the trunk and to take them and graft them on to other trunks so if the root does perish, he'll still have the fruit from the tree.[9]

The servant does as he is ordered, and the master again prunes, digs about the roots, and nourishes the original tree. The master then takes the shoots from the original tree and grafts them into various

8 Book of Mormon, Jacob 5:3–6.

9 Ibid., Jacob 5:7–8.

trees around the edges of the vineyard, so hopefully he won't lose both the tree and the fruits.[10]

A long time passes, and the Lord of the vineyard decides to go see what is happening in the vineyard. He finds that the original tree, with the branches from the wild olive tree, is now beginning to bear fruit. "And he beheld that it was good, and the fruit thereof was like unto the natural fruit."[11] They have saved the tree, and the strength of the roots is such that the wild branches have brought forth tame fruit. The master and the servant go and check on all the shoots from the original tree to see how they're doing. The first one has flourished and is covered with fruit. The servant asks, "Why did you plant here? This is the poorest spot in all the land of thy vineyard."

The response to the servant's question is as follows, from Jacob 5:22–26:

> 22 And the Lord of the vineyard said unto him: 'Counsel me not; I knew that it was a poor spot of ground; wherefore, I said unto thee, I have nourished it this long time, and thou beholdest that it hath brought forth much fruit.' . . .
>
> 25 And he said unto the servant: 'Look hither and behold the last. Behold, this have I planted in a good spot of ground; and I have nourished it this long time, and only a part of the tree hath brought forth tame fruit, and the other part of the tree hath brought forth wild fruit; behold, I have nourished this tree like unto the others.'
>
> 26 And it came to pass that the Lord of the vineyard said unto the servant: 'Pluck off the branches that have not brought forth good fruit, and cast them into the fire.'

We have a vineyard in this story, with a focus on one particular tree, and the struggle to get the fruits of that tree. When the tree starts to die, new shoots from wild trees are grafted in to the original rootstock, and shoots from the original tree are planted in other parts of the vineyard, some in poor soil and others in good soil. Some of the branches and shoots bear good fruit, and others do not. When the master of the vineyard gets frustrated with the poor fruits, he's ready to cut off the branches and burn them.

But the servant says, "Let's try pruning, digging about it, and nourishing it a little longer." So they prune and dig about, and

---

10 Book of Mormon, Jacob 5:9–14.
11 Ibid., Jacob 5:17.

nourish all the trees in the vineyard. And then they go away. And after a long time they come back to check on the trees. They visit each of the trees, and to make a long story short, all the trees are now bearing bad fruits.

Again from the book of Jacob Chapter 5:

> 41 And it came to pass that the Lord of the vineyard wept, and said unto the servant: 'What could I have done more for my vineyard? . . .
>
> 47 Have I slackened mine hand, that I have not nourished it? Nay, I have nourished it, and I have digged about it, and I have pruned it, and I have dunged it; and I have stretched forth mine hand almost all the day long, and the end draweth nigh. And it grieveth me that I should hew down all the trees of my vineyard, and cast them into the fire that they should be burned. Who is it that has corrupted my vineyard?

The servant again convinces the master not to chop down and burn the trees, but rather to bring the original shoots back and put them on the original rootstock. They continue this back and forth through several cycles, nourishing, pruning, loosening the soil, and the end of the story is a triumph of the natural branches and a return to the original, good fruits of the tree.

Both of these stories are of the pursuit of fruitfulness for a specific tree. The stories are rich with images. The wild tree, the tame tree, the Jewish/Gentile dichotomy that Paul sets up, the one who does the grafting, the movement of the shoots to different environments in search of the right place for those shoots, the growing edges, the process of grafting, and the fruits of the tame tree.

Let's start with the wild olive tree. Paul sees it as a combination of not being Jewish and not following God's teachings. In the book of Jacob, the wild olive tree is from outside the vineyard where God's people are growing. Robert Barclay, an early Quaker writer, has another image — that of our own first fallen nature. In Barclay's *Apology for the True Christian Divinity*,[12] first published in 1678, he gives us fifteen propositions that provide a theological explication and justification for the Quaker tradition. The tenth proposition

---

12 Robert Barclay, *An Apology for the True Christian Divinity* (Farmington, ME: Quaker Heritage Press edition, 2002).

focuses on ministry, which might also be heard as fruitfulness. "To be a member then of the catholic church, there is a need of the *inward calling of God* by his Light in the heart, and a being leavened into the nature and spirit of it, so as to forsake unrighteousness and be turned to righteousness, and, in the inwardness of the mind, to be cut out of the wild olive tree of our own first fallen nature and ingrafted into Christ by his Word and Spirit in the heart."[13] To Barclay the catholic church is the spiritual community that welcomes all who hear and heed the promptings of the still small voice, that of God within each of us.

So what is the wild olive tree of our first fallen nature? Some of us might reject those terms as being reminiscent of original sin. But there is a truth in the tendency to live our lives at a distance from the Spirit. And that first fallen nature can be seen as the human instincts, the natural man, the self-centeredness we can all use to blind ourselves to the Inward Teacher. Sit with the image for yourself. What have you been cut out of, and what do you need to be cut out of to be fully grafted in to the Divine Source?

The Divine Source is one way of understanding the tame tree. Barclay explicitly refers to the "ingrafting into Christ by his Word and Spirit in the heart."[14] We can describe that rootstock more universally as the Christ Spirit that walks fully in the Divine Presence and the human world simultaneously, who invites each of us to do the same. Paul's story of grafting includes the naming of the understock as the Jews, the chosen people, and the scion as the Gentiles.

Many religious traditions lift up the members of their community as the chosen people. Everyone who has felt called by the Divine Spirit has rested in the uniqueness of the call, calling forth the fruits we have been created to bear. I believe every religious tradition originates with an interaction, a breaking open of the walls between human and Divine. And into the uniqueness of the breaking open comes the human need to feel special, singled out, unique. We superimpose the limits of our human comprehension on the divine interaction, and we build a theology, worldview, and organizational structure on the interaction. The limited capacity of our human minds cannot comprehend how God's unique call could go out to

13 Barclay, p. 233.
14 Barclay, loc. cit.

each and every human heart. One of the many fruits of the Quaker tree is the understanding there is that of God in each of us, and God's universal but unique invitation can be experienced in each human heart. The chosen are not chosen by God — we are *all* chosen by God. Our role is to respond to the invitation: Do we choose God? Paul is absolutely correct in challenging the branches to remain faithful and humble, because in his story they could always be cut off. The challenge for us is to hear the Truth of the image underlying the ethnocentric overlay of Jewish superiority. What does it mean to be cut off from the tame tree?

The one doing the grafting in Paul is unknown — the branches were grafted in, with no named actor responsible. The Book of Mormon, on the other hand, has two clear actors: the Lord of the vineyard and his servant. The presence of these two figures in the Book of Mormon story adds the dimension of the feelings of the Lord and servant of the vineyard as they struggle to encourage the fruitfulness of the tree.

The presence of one who does the grafting, and who selects the location where a particular shoot will be grafted, encourages us to consider Divine Providence in our lives. Can we have faith we've been put some place where that Providence hopes we'll be fruitful? Sometimes we aren't fruitful and need to be moved to another location to see if we'll be fruitful there. The story from the book of Jacob also includes the movement of the shoots to different parts of the vineyard, seeking to find an environment where each shoot will be able to bear the fruits they were intended to bear. While I grew up Mormon, I felt there were fruits I could not bring forth in that tradition. I hold the Divine motion in my move to Quakerism.

The image of the shoots being moved to different places in the vineyard is both an opportunity and a challenge. Shoots were placed in poor soil and were able to bear fruit. Shoots were placed in rich soil and brought forth bad fruit. This image challenges me to accept my own responsibility for bearing fruit and challenges me to grow into the rootstock where I am. Another image I take from the moving around of the shoots, is that when we come into a particular place, or a particular religious tradition, we need to pay attention to where the cambium, our growing edge, is placed so we can be grafted in. Where is the cambium in the Quaker tradition?

Both of these stories include the grafting, the growing together, of shoots and rootstock. And we need to attend to the growing edge in each of us, and the care that needs to be taken with that growing edge. Our lives are a process of making and breaking connections with those things in this world that feed our souls and those things in this world that keep us too closely tied to our lesser selves. It is important to understand that we are surrounded and embedded in more visible rootstock, and most of us are in the process of putting down roots and growing into a multitude of traditions. Sometimes the rootstocks are things we inadvertently grow into — the rules and regulations of our culture and society that we unconsciously breathe in and accept, and the guidelines of our religious traditions which tell us how God works and does not work.

One of the most vigorous rootstocks is the culture around us. In August 2007 at New England Yearly Meeting annual sessions, the keynote speaker, Duduzile Mtshazo (from South Africa) shared a story of a time she realized how thoroughly she'd been grafted into the culture of apartheid. She told us of going to get the plane ticket for her first flight out of South Africa. The airline office was in a round building, and she walked around the building multiple times looking for a sign to let her know which door she should go in, as a black person. There was no sign. This story illustrates how we need to be careful in our lives what we put our cambium, our growing edge, in contact with. We need to try to see the patterns that shape our world view that we have internalized because of the culture that we are rooted in.

There are numerous queries that grow out of these two stories of grafting. I offer a number of queries below, and I encourage you to walk with the queries that speak to you.

Quakerism strives to welcome newcomers, and I believe it has played the important role of offering a religious tradition that can be a haven for refugees from other religions. Participation in the life of a Quaker meeting rarely distinguishes between members who have formally joined and attenders. This welcoming is a strength and a weakness — a strength as it welcomes and encourages participation of all, and a weakness in that it can dilute the Quaker grounding of the community. To maintain the Quaker tradition in an open and welcoming congregation, I believe we need to challenge ourselves and each other to be fully grafted into the Quaker tradition. Only with a strong ground in the Quaker rootstock will a community be able to support the branches and fruits that those coming to Quaker meetings hunger for.

Queries

Am I being faithful where I am?

What is the rootstock that nurtures me?

What am I being grafted into?

Where are my growing edges?

What do I need to be cut off from?

What rootstock supports my spiritual journey?

When have I been fruitful in poor soil?

When have I been unfruitful in good soil?

CHAPTER 8

Engaging with a Monthly Meeting about Ministry

This essay is written by Debbie Humphries and Diane Randall.

What does it mean to be called to public ministry within the Religious Society of Friends?

What does it mean to submit to the discipline of the corporate community?

What can monthly meetings do to respond to individual leadings of ministry?

The Call (Debbie)

As New England Yearly Meeting gathered for its 350th annual sessions in August 1999 in a momentous visit to the historic Newport Meetinghouse, I found myself shaking and felt the Spirit moving. This is the message that came through me: "As Quakers we have a powerful heritage, but today we are a pale shadow of who we are called to be. The world needs what we hold, and we need to come forward and live faithfully to the Spirit and to the Quaker tradition."

The experience was transformative. The call I felt began an internal struggle to understand the Spirit's work in my life. Over the following years, I grew into a deeper understanding of Quakerism, ministry, and my own sense of call. The treasures in the Quaker tradition became alive to me in its rich history. I cultivated space in my life to listen and practice the skills of discernment as well as how to hear how the Spirit calls me. Another treasure in the Quaker tradition is the knowledge that listening alone, we may misunderstand what the Spirit is asking. When others from our spiritual community listen with us we can be more confident that we are listening to that inner guide and not our own ego.

Following yearly meeting sessions in 1999, I continued to feel closer to the Spirit than I ever had by reading Quaker books, studying and meditating. Books that told the lives and stories of historic Friends such as Daisy Newman's *A Procession of Friends*, John Punshon's *Encounter with Silence*, George Fox's *Journal*, John Woolman's autobiography, Rebecca Larson's *Daughters of Light*, and Samuel Bownas's *Description of the Qualifications Necessary to a Gospel Minister* made me aware of a sense of power and truth in this faith tradition that I hadn't felt among contemporary Friends. I was moved by the stirrings of the Spirit in the lives and writings of so many Friends.

In the fall of 2000, I began a year of monthly personal retreats (described in Chapter 4, "A Listening Year"), usually for twenty-four hours of silence, reflection, journaling, reading and worship. My purpose was for time alone to come to know what the moving of the Spirit felt like outside of meeting for worship. That fall I also sought guidance from three seasoned Friends in our meetings to meet with me on an ad hoc (but regular) basis. My request to them was to help me keep from running ahead or behind my leading. As the ad hoc committee's understanding of my ministry and the corporate accountability I was seeking for the ministry grew, the committee began to see itself more as a support committee.

Samuel Bownas's *Description of the Qualifications of a Gospel Minister* led me to wonder about asking my monthly meeting for help in living the ministry I am called to. Bownas described clearly the growth and changes I was experiencing, naming the ministry I felt called to not as a gift to the individual, but to the meeting.

Because of my leading to travel to other meetings, I wanted my monthly meeting to accept and provide oversight for my ministry. I had a hunger to share the weight of the leading and I sought help from the meeting as a whole. I learned about current practices among Friends who recognize the distinction between a support committee, which acknowledges the ministry of the individual, and an oversight committee, where the meeting accepts some responsibility for nurturing the ministry. I also struggled with ego, not wanting to suggest my ministry was more important or special than the ministries of others.

In October 2001, I wrote to the Worship & Ministry Committee of Hartford Monthly Meeting:

> In August of this year while we were traveling . . . I was moved to
> speak, and now I feel the need to prepare for when it will be time to

visit other meetings on an intentional basis, rather than just convenience. It's not yet time, but I am listening and waiting. And as I prepare for this, I am asking for the meeting to accept responsibility of oversight of my call to vocal ministry. I do not consider this a confidential matter, but rather a sacred matter to be discussed and shared in the Light.

I would describe my ministry/leading as follows: I am led to call others to a deepening of their faith. This necessitates a continual deepening of my own faith, as I strive to listen to the Presence I feel and give myself over to it.

The Meeting's Response (Diane)

To determine the best way to respond to Debbie's request, Worship and Ministry contacted other meetings to ask about their support and oversight committees. In January 2002, they made the following recommendation to Meeting for Business:

> . . . that a committee of oversight be appointed to help provide clarity and guidance to the faithful exercise of the gifts of ministry coming through Debbie Humphries. Debbie feels called by an acute awareness of historical strength and power provided by the witness of the Society of Friends, and by a corresponding sense that Friends are called to be more than we currently are in the world today. A clearness committee under Worship & Ministry finds Debbie clear to pursue this ministry.

The concept of a committee of oversight for an individual's ministry was unfamiliar — to our Worship and Ministry Committee, to me as a new clerk, and to many in our unprogrammed meeting. At that business meeting, we did not find unity to support the request for oversight.

Over time, Debbie's request led Hartford Monthly Meeting to examine the idea of "ministry" as an individual call and to consider our meeting's responsibility to an individual's leading. We did this in structured gatherings to read and reflect together and in conversations with one another. We grappled with many questions, such as: How do we define and understand Debbie's ministry? If the meeting has oversight, does that mean Debbie will be speaking for our meeting? Aren't we all ministers? If we recognize Debbie's gift of ministry as unique or needing special attention, what does that say about the rest of us as ministers? Will providing "oversight" mean we have financial responsibility for Debbie and her family? Isn't ministry usually what we call messages in worship from older, seasoned Friends?

Although Debbie had been worshipping with Friends for ten years and held membership in Charleston (West Virginia) Monthly Meeting, she had been attending Hartford Monthly Meeting for only three years when she asked for our Meeting's oversight. Some people in the Meeting simply didn't feel they knew Debbie well enough, nor did they understand how to define her ministry.

At our May, 2002 Meeting for Business, our worship together resulted in a process minute:

> The request for an oversight committee for Debbie Humphries' ministry, . . . has offered fertile ground for exploring gifts, leadings and ministry within Hartford Monthly Meeting. Through structured discussion and worship, we have listened to one another and to God. These opportunities have included a Sunday morning Eleventh Hour and a Saturday morning Books and Bagels discussion; a workshop exploring gifts and leadings led by Charlotte Fardelmann; in worship sharing with Charlotte on the topic of how the community supports leadings; [as well as] in-worship sharing with Brian Drayton on the topic of vocal ministry and deepening the life of the Meeting. Hartford Friends earnestly desire and actively work to support one another. This mutual support is borne out in countless ways. And yet, this request for oversight of ministry seems to engage us in a new way that is not yet clear; we have struggled with understanding what Debbie's ministry is and what "oversight" means. In June, the Committees of Pastoral Care and Worship and Ministry will continue their discussion on the role of the faith community in nurturing leadings and ministries, and the role of the individual to the faith community.

In September 2002, at a specially called meeting for business, the meeting affirmed the gift of ministry:

> Clerk Diane Randall opened the meeting with a statement of our purpose of Loving one another.
>
> Friends wrestled deeply and prayerfully with questions of authority and the concept of meeting oversight, recognizing our own fears and doubts. We are clear that at any time any of us may be

called to a particular form of ministry. Friends expressed concerns and had questions about what it means for a called minister to "go out" in the name of a particular meeting. We also prayerfully considered the meaning of ministry. How do we define ministry? We recognize that within the Society of Friends has been a long tradition of ministry[;] how does this relate to our own meeting, to our own calls? We recognize that none of us speaks in vocal ministry on behalf of our Meeting, but as one who has listened closely to that [which] the Spirit is asking.

★ ★ ★ ★

We are clear that Debbie is felt [sic] called to her ministry. We want to support this. We recognize her reaching out to our Meeting, as she has stated, is a call for support and to help her "not outrun" her leadings. We wrestled with the issue of whether an oversight committee gives authority to Debbie to speak on behalf of the Meeting.

Such a committee would be a way for Debbie to test her leadings within its loving and safe community and help offer guidance to insure her outward work stays true and accountable to that to which she is called.

Friends entered into a period of silent worship. After deep and heartfelt comments were heard, recognizing the concerns of some around the balance of giving ministerial support to all of our members and our not having clarity on some issues around ministerial oversight, we were clear that we need to continue to support Debbie's leadings, though we are not clear at this time to support the appointment of an oversight committee. At this time, Debbie's support will come through her Support Committee, working with Worship and Ministry, which will continue to advise our Meeting and to further nurture her gifts.

Spiritual growth (Debbie)

Following the called meeting for business, people were concerned about my feelings; however, I didn't feel the decision was personal. The meeting was acting on faith and was not prepared to accept corporate responsibility for the leadings of individual members. I had been faithful because the ministry I'm called to does not belong to me — it is the work of the Spirit. I am not responsible for removing the roadblocks in my path — I can only express my willingness to the Spirit to continue the ministry, and ask to make the way clear.

I continued having regular meetings with my support committee, which has seen a change in members over the years. They have been critical in challenging me, listening with me, and accompanying me on this journey. They encouraged me to write down the vocal ministry I was given, and those messages are an important part of what I know. They encouraged me to say yes to New England Yearly Meeting committee service. They gently fed back my own foibles and helped me grow through them. This is, of course, an ongoing task! Writing monthly reports has been an important discipline, as I take the time to reflect on how the ministry is moving.

The spiritual formation through the Meeting's labor (Diane)

Debbie's personal leading and engagement of our meeting's corporate support required us to consider how God calls us — and how we understand these calls as ministry. Through examining questions of ministry concerning Debbie, we began asking ourselves and each other, "Is all of our work 'ministry'?" Our meeting is filled with individuals who labor on behalf of a better world and exercise their spiritual gifts — in their homes, their professional lives and in our meeting. The variety of service we do — working to end homelessness, offering dignity and aid to people with mental illness and HIV/AIDS, teaching students of all ages, protecting the environment, promoting civil rights, organizing against the United States' engagement in torture, fighting racism and homophobia, volunteering in prisons, promoting peace education, creating art, caring for aging parents and older members of meeting and nurturing children — is this all Spirit-led?

Over time, we began to lose the constraints of the words "minister" and "oversight." Debbie's regular interaction with people who served on her support committee led them to know her deeply. She met with anyone who didn't understand her leading. As Debbie became better known in our monthly and yearly meetings, contributing her time and skills in a way that demonstrated her commitment and leadership, Friends felt easier with the idea of Debbie "traveling in the ministry."

In October, 2004 with the endorsement of her support committee, the meeting considered Debbie's letter of request for a travel minute. Grounded in historical practice and prayerful consideration of elders in the meeting, the request gave the background and purpose for travel minutes, as well as a description of accountability to the meeting.

> The purpose of a travel minute is to indicate that the leading of the Friend who carries it has been recognized by the home meeting, and that she travels among Friends with our corporate support. Travel minutes are discussed in Faith and Practice (p. 264–65). . . . As my leading is to travel both within and outside of New England Yearly Meeting, if Hartford Meeting approves the minute, I will then take it to Connecticut Valley Quarterly Meeting and New England Yearly Meeting for their endorsement.
>
> A travel minute is used to introduce an individual and [her] ministry to other communities of Friends. After a visit, a travel minute is endorsed by the visited meeting, and those comments can then be shared with the home meeting. I will make a yearly report to the meeting on the work done with this travel minute.
>
> I feel led to travel both within New England Yearly Meeting and outside. I anticipate traveling with other Friends, as this ministry is best done with a companion.

At that meeting, Hartford Monthly Meeting approved providing a travel minute, which was written by then Clerk Cynthia Reik:

> To Friends in New England and elsewhere:
>
> We commend to you our beloved Friend, Debbie Humphries, whose leading to travel in the ministry has been seasoned in Hartford Monthly Meeting. We recognize her call to travel among Friends as the Spirit leads, to join them in fellowship, worship and prayer.
>
> Her concern is to deepen the spiritual life of the Religious Society of Friends, to re-awaken us to experience the vitality and power of the Spirit, and to remind Friends of the truths of our tradition. Her faithfulness to this call has been an ongoing source of spiritual nourishment for her, our Meeting and beyond. Debbie has served on many committees within our meeting and also on several committees of New England Yearly Meeting. In all of these works Debbie's gifts of discernment, faithfulness to the traditions of Friends as well as listening and counsel have increased.

We encourage her in this response to what we discern to be the promptings of love and truth, trusting that, under the Lord's hand, and with the prayers of Friends, her service among you will be faithful and fruitful.

With Debbie we send our loving greetings to all Friends whom she may encounter.

Ongoing Travels (Debbie)

From 2004 to 2013 I visited more than sixty meetings, often experiencing a grace that gave me words to speak to the condition of individuals and meetings. I believe that grace is in part due to Hartford Monthly Meeting's support. When I visit a worshiping community, I come into the worship in a much deeper way because I am carrying my meeting's endorsement.

The process that I have used in traveling in the ministry is to write to monthly meetings, asking for an opportunity to visit. I gather with them in worship outside of their regularly scheduled meeting for worship, often meeting with a small group on a Saturday evening and then attending Meeting for Worship on First Day. Spending worship sharing time with a smaller group from the meeting deepens the regular worship the next morning.

As a way to share my travels and the accountability for the ministry, I write a report annually to Hartford Meeting, which is read in Meeting for Business, along with endorsements from visited meetings and sometimes a written report from my support committee.

In each of my visits, the vocal ministry has varied, but the underlying theme always returns to attending to our Quaker heritage, listening to what it has to teach us, and learning to live more faithfully as Quakers today. The treasures of our faith tradition can help us respond to the world around us, if we practice our disciplines of listening and individual and corporate discernment.

Every day we make decisions about how we will act. Quaker faith and practice holds the hope of clarity on every aspect of our lives — from the small daily decisions to the large life decisions. One of the promises of Quakerism is an answer to the question "What am I called to do?" The emphasis on individual ministry and discernment is strengthened by the tradition of corporate listening, where we discern together how the Spirit is calling us.

We're all called to ministry. Not all of us are called to be a preacher, or called to speak in meeting. Rather, we understand ministry as the work to build the peaceable kingdom, and each one of us has a part to play. Whatever we're doing, when we're doing the work of the Spirit it is ministry. Each of us has a ministry and our worshiping community can serve to strengthen us in carrying out our own ministry.

Queries

How do you seek support for the ministry you carry?

When have you submitted to the discipline and guidance of your meeting or worshiping community?

CHAPTER 9

Four Pillars of
Meeting for Business

IN MAY 2007, the board of the School of the Spirit Ministries, on
which I was serving, was in the process of discerning whether to
add a new program. We had a very intense one-and-a-half-day meeting, which resulted in the decision to move forward with a new
program, which became The Way of Ministry. At the end of a long
Saturday, I headed to Philadelphia's 30th Street Station to catch a train
home to Hartford. I knew I was to speak the next morning at the
Unitarian Universalist Society of Greater Hartford, and they had
asked me to give a presentation on Quaker business practice. Sitting
in the station, I was inspired to write down four key components of
Quaker corporate discernment, using examples from the board of
School of the Spirit Ministries discernment experience, which then
formed the backbone of my presentation.

Over the next year I carried these four components, and I have
continued to grow in my understanding of each of them. As I have
sat with Friends in corporate discernment and visited meetings in
New England, I have come to believe we need to revisit the practice
of corporate discernment. The form of Quaker business practice is a
rich process which at its best builds community, changes hearts, and
unites us with the Spirit, despite differences of opinion. We need to
refresh our understanding of our purpose and our practices, and seek
to hold them more deeply, to bring ourselves more fully into alignment with God's purpose in our lives.

At the heart of Quakerism is the sentiment that there is "that of
God in every one." Quakers repeat this phrase to try to describe the
core we share. Embedded in it is the belief that the good — which is
that of God — can be raised up in each of us. As early Quaker theolo-
gian Robert Barclay described his experience of worship with Friends:

> "When I came into the silent assemblies of God's people, I felt a
> secret power amongst them which touched my heart; and as I gave

way unto it, I found the evil weakening in me, and the good raised up and so I became thus knit and united unto them, hungering more and more after the increase of this power and life, whereby I might find myself perfectly redeemed."[1]

The potential of attending to the secret power, of listening in the silence, of giving way to the power and finding the evil weakening and the good raised up, is foundational to all branches of Quakerism.

The Quaker tradition challenges us to relate to others in ways which call forth and resonate with the good within them, however deeply it may be buried. Quakerism is an optimistic tradition, as we believe hearts can change and the good can be raised up. The potential for growth in the Spirit is there for each of us. Our worship and our business practice, at their core, are about creating the conditions for hearts to change. By using these corporate practices we are also learning how to act toward others in ways which honor that of God in them.

As I have visited Quaker meetings, I have observed Friends faithfully following the form of Quaker business practices without necessarily understanding the importance and purpose of the form. George Fox challenged the people around him to seek the power rather than the form. He condemned many as engaged in religious practices which were empty forms, where people followed their practices without understanding the deeper meaning and so had lost contact with the meaning. Accepting the responsibility to keep Quaker and other faith traditions living and vibrant requires that we work to understand why we use the forms we do, so the practices are not empty but rich with life. Within the Quaker practice of corporate discernment there is a treasure the world needs. It is a way of coming together as individuals with different experiences, needs, agendas, and perspectives and engaging with each other to strengthen relationships and make decisions affecting the community.

The pillars that I see undergirding the forms of Quaker business practice are the following:

- the meeting is rooted in worship;
- the meeting is clerked;

---

1 Robert Barclay, *Apology for the True Christian Divinity*, first published in 1678 (Farmington, ME: Quaker Heritage Press), p. 300)

- there is enough time, a sense of spaciousness; and
- decisions are made by sense of the meeting.

Meeting for Business is Grounded in Worship

Every business meeting begins with a time of worship. At times the worship is perfunctory, but at its best, the opening worship is long enough to remind those present that we are listening deeply and seeking to hear the Spirit in the agenda items addressed.

The entire meeting for business is the corporate implementation of the skills developed in meeting for worship. Each time we sit together with others in corporate worship, we have the opportunity to further develop these skills. Some of them are at the individual level, where each of us needs to develop our inward ear, the ear of our heart. Building upon the individual skills are the corporate ones of listening together for something more than what we hear individually. Both the individual and corporate skills can be understood as queries such as, Can I hear God / Spirit in my heart? Do I know what it feels like to hear God in my heart? When I listen, can I tell the difference between my own ego and the Inward Teacher?

Early in my journey into Quakerism, after having a powerful experience of being called to ministry, I called together a support committee of three seasoned Friends to sit with me to provide some guidance so I didn't run ahead of — or behind — my leading. Shortly after they came together, I was led to commit to monthly retreats for nine months. My children were three and five years old, so it was no small feat to make time to go away one weekend a month. The support and understanding of my husband, John, made it possible.

I met with the support committee right before my first retreat, and they asked what my focus was for the retreat. Tears came to my eyes as I told them I didn't know how to hear God except when I was moved to speak in meeting for worship. My hope for the personal retreats was to be able to come to know the Spirit: to recognize it when I felt it, and to be able to hear it when I stopped to listen. The retreats were at different locations — a Benedictine Abbey in Connecticut, a Quaker conference center in Massachusetts, a friend's home on Block Island in Rhode Island — but at each place I would look for a comfortable armchair beside a window and spend a lot of time sitting comfortably there. The silent time was where I became aware of the physical sensations that accompany my attending to the Light within.

The lesson of discerning when my ego is talking is one I have not learned easily, and I have to relearn this lesson time and again. I remember one particular business session at New England Yearly Meeting where the lesson came home strongly. I knew the session was going to be long, although I couldn't have predicted how few people walked out even when we were over an hour and a half late in completing the business. During the evening session I groaned internally when someone repeated what another had already said, or when a speaker was going on at what I thought was excessive length, or when a speaker didn't appear to be listening to what others had said. I came to the realization early on that all of these internal criticisms were my own ego, and I committed right then to lifting those internal voices up and letting them go. I listened deeply that night, holding the business in my heart, feeling deep warmth in my belly, and knowing we were exactly where we needed to be as a worshiping community. The experience helped me name the voice of my own ego.

The touchstone for discerning Spirit and ego in my own experience is the love which will fill any motion that starts with Spirit. And the love will be for all. The voice which holds up honor and respect for each of us is more likely to be Spirit than a voice which diminishes the worth of another. Paul provides his own guidance for this same discernment when he says, "But the fruit of the Spirit is love, joy, peace, patience, kindness, goodness, faithfulness, gentleness, and self-control." (Gal. 5:22)

When Do I Hear Spirit Moving in the Silence?

Quakerism is about listening in silence. Early Friends spoke about what happened in the silence and focused much less on the content of vocal ministry. It was in the silence their hearts were broken open. As Robert Barclay describes it:

> Yea, though there be not a word spoken, yet is the true spiritual worship performed, and the body of Christ edified; yea, it may, and hath often fallen out among us, that divers meetings have passed without one word; and yet our souls have been greatly edified and refreshed,

and our hearts wonderfully overcome with the secret sense of God's power and Spirit, which without words hath been ministered from one vessel to another.[2]

We need a vocabulary to describe the different textures of our corporate silence so we can better appreciate the experience. When we focus on the vocal ministry to evaluate the quality of our corporate worship we have looked to the fruits and missed the source. Attending to the quality of the corporate silence can disentangle the personal issues which arise in reacting to the vocal ministry of another. Sometimes our experience in the silence might be fragmented, distracted, or scattered, with our thoughts and focus jumping from one thing to another. Other times it might be a deep stillness where many of those present feel held to attention, perhaps like what happens in a yoga asana where the breath moves through us while the mind is quiet. Practice can help us come to the place of deep, focused attentiveness more readily.

We practice listening to the Spirit in meeting for worship. It is important to also practice listening individually, on a daily basis. A regular spiritual practice such as daily prayer time, a journal, walks in nature, or Scripture reading can help us tune the inward ear to God's presence. Meeting for worship is an opportunity to practice corporate tuning and listening, without the additional challenge of decision-making that is present in meeting for business. We need to develop the skills of listening in the silence for the Spirit, to know when the silence is rich and deep, and to feel when the silence is scattered, disjointed, and not yet gathered. Then we will understand that the quality of Quaker worship is about much more than the messages.

When do I hear Spirit in the ministry of others?

Can I hear the spirit of the messages of others, the Spirit underlying the words?

The work of listening, the capacity to distinguish between when something is only "a good idea" and when it is the Spirit moving, is fundamental to Quaker business practice. We work on the listening corporately every week in worship, hoping for the grace of a "gathered" meeting, where we feel the Spirit knitting us together. This is

2 Barclay, *Apology*, p. 296.

not an easy listening, and it is an extension of the earlier exercise of being aware of our own ego. I have visited meetings where the Spirit was powerfully present in the ministry, even though messages felt longer than needed and there wasn't as much silence and worshipful space surrounding the messages as I would have liked. If I had stayed with my impatience over the length of the messages and the lack of silence, I would have missed the very real presence and movement of the Spirit.

One of the challenges in learning to listen deeply to the Spirit in worship and silence is Quakers seldom intentionally create opportunities to check with others about what we heard in worship, and to receive feedback on our sense of when the Spirit is moving and when it is not. We need to create more opportunities to work on our worship skills — to talk about, practice, and then discuss the experience. The skills of discernment and listening we practice in meeting for worship are essential for the corporate business practice. Being grounded in worship is critical. If the worshipful environment changes or discussion becomes heated, the clerk may ask for silence to give those present the time to go back to worshipful space. Centering in the silence can help us be tender with the agendas of others, and be more aware of our own.

Meeting for Business Is Clerked

Each meeting for business has an individual who has been named to clerk the meeting. The clerk's work includes visible and invisible tasks. The former includes preparing the agenda, calling on people to speak, and giving voice to a sense of the meeting for those present to respond to. The latter includes the prayer and discernment which go into preparing the agenda, being in a grounded and centered place from which to attend to the motion of Spirit in the corporate body during the conduct of business, and hearing what is not said but is present in the room.

The visible tasks are not necessarily simple. In most meetings, the clerk is responsible for identifying agenda items and discerning the order in which to consider those items. The order of the agenda can be important: for instance, addressing difficult items — the ones where discussion might be tense — closer to the beginning of the meeting, when people are fresh and may be more focused. The clerk is also responsible for recognizing individuals before they speak. This can be a very important practice of discernment, as Jan Hoffman demonstrated during her time clerking New England Yearly Meeting when she listened inwardly to discern who to call on next. This is an important tool allowing clerks to wait and feel the inward motion, reminding the body over and over of the importance of the posture of deep listening. Clerks of New England Yearly Meeting continue to use this practice. A clerk can also make use of the process of recognizing someone to speak to call the group into waiting worship until the Spirit is ready.

In business meeting, speakers address their remarks to the clerk. This allows a little more space for Friends to not feel directly attacked by someone else's differing opinion, and to listen better to perspectives which differ from their own. This can help Friends disentangle their ego's stake in an issue and instead listen to the guidance of the Spirit, and be open to letting go of their own position. At times when the business is focusing on questions of clarification or when the business before the group is easily agreed upon, the clerk's role may seem less critical, but even then these disciplines are important because the practice of being recognized by the clerk and speaking to the clerk needs to be second nature in times of tension and disagreement.

The invisible tasks of the clerk help to hold a worshipful space and remind those present of the importance of listening to the Spirit. Praying about the agenda, about which items to include, whether to hold an item over to another meeting, and how best to prepare the meeting for a particular business item can undergird the business meeting with an invisible sense of Spirit.

The first time I went to a meeting of New England Yearly Meeting's Ministry and Counsel, I was deeply moved by the clerking. Cornelia Parkes maintained a presence free of anxiety despite an overfull agenda. She had clearly prepared well; she knew the agenda items and people involved well enough to rearrange the agenda when needed, to attend to each business item gently and faithfully, and to keep us in a listening space as needed to move through the work people had gathered to complete.

One of the important practices of a clerk is being a non-anxious presence. This is a challenge for many of us. When a situation gets tense, we may become reactive rather than remaining deeply rooted in our own sense of Spirit. When disagreement or strong feelings are present, the greatest hope for change comes when someone is able to remain in a place of centered calm. This does not mean disengaging from the process or from those present. Instead, it means being able to hold the tension of others without catching it or needing to release it. When we merely avoid tension, we limit our ability to face conflict and to enable transformation from the tension. In contrast, staying in a place of conflict in a respectful and centered way, knowing we need inspiration to resolve the conflict, releases the full transformative potential of meeting for business and increases the likelihood those present will be able to hear and respond to the motion of the Spirit.

Business Meeting Will Have Enough Time

Quakers make jokes about how long the business process can take, generally without realizing what takes so long is for hearts to change. It is difficult for most of us to admit publicly we are wrong, especially when we have spoken strongly about a topic. This can take a long time, particularly since we may not consciously realize we're waiting for those present to release their ego-centered opinions — including our own. Changing hearts is eased when we all can discern the source of the words which come to us and to others. Quaker business practice is about speaking our own Light on the subject, and then setting aside our own perspective to listen to the moving of the Spirit.

At its best, Quaker business practice carries a sense of spaciousness: the search for the right outcome will take as long as it needs to. There is enough space for people to bring and share their opinions, hesitations, and concerns; and because they will not be attacked for their perspectives, or challenged directly and personally, there is a potential for movement.

In the School of the Spirit Ministries board meeting, where the decision was made to move forward with the Way of Ministry Program, several board members expressed deep concerns about the additional financial burdens and oversight responsibilities for a new program. No one expressed the perspective that initiating a new program would be easy. We held the concerns about the board being too small, and we waited for the Spirit. When we found clarity, it was with a decision to move forward in faith, trusting way would open and the necessary resources would be found.

I visited a meeting some years ago whose members were struggling with questions about their meeting space — whether they should seek another space, build an extension, or build a new meetinghouse. They were in the stage of gathering information and identifying and costing out the alternatives. The meeting was carefully following Quaker process, bringing the alternatives forward. However, the meeting was a young meeting — not in age, or even in experience with Quaker organizations, but in having limited experience diving fully into the Quaker tradition as a guide for individual spirituality. I was led to remind them when the time came to make a decision, they needed to release their own opinions of the best option so they could be open to how they might be led by the Spirit.

Business Meeting Decisions Will Be by Sense of the Meeting

One of the assumptions in Quaker business practice is something more than the best wisdom of the group will be achieved — those present are listening for something more than what each person thinks. Working toward a sense of the meeting is about listening for what Spirit would have us do in this instance. It is not a negotiated settlement or compromise, giving each person some of what they want. Rather, it is a moving toward, which does not require logical agreement. Barry Morley's Pendle Hill Pamphlet, "Beyond Consensus: Salvaging a Sense of the Meeting,"[3] is a wonderful description and invitation into the power of waiting and listening for a sense of the meeting. One of the powerful examples from Hartford Monthly Meeting of a clear sense of the meeting was when we decided to install a lift in the meetinghouse. Two options were presented at a special meeting for business, with the price tag for one being more than double that of the other. The lower cost option would add the lift on at the end of our building; the higher cost option had the lift right beside one of the main entrances. As we sat in business meeting, people spoke to concerns about the cost, and whether it was really

---

3 *Beyond Consensus: Salvaging a Sense of the Meeting*, Pendle Hill Pamphlet # 307 (Wallingtford, PA: Pendle Hill, 1993).

needed. And then a friend spoke to how welcoming it would be to someone who needed to use the lift to have the lift right beside the main entrance, in contrast to the "tacked on" feel of the cheaper option at the back of the meeting house. We settled into waiting worship, and hearts were changed. We were united in our sense that the lift needed to be by the main entrance even though it came with the much higher price tag. The clerk gave voice to the sense of the meeting, and those present approved the minute.

At its best, Quaker business builds the worshiping community, strengthens relationships, and encourages each of us to grow. It holds space for individual and community transformation grounded in love. When our corporate decisions are faithful to this Spirit, they not only change the participants; they hold the seeds that change the world.

Queries

Are you listening for the Spirit in meeting for business?

When you listen in meeting for business can you distinguish between your ego and the Inward Teacher?

CHAPTER 10

Embracing Wholeness
in the World

An earlier version of this talk was given as an invited plenary talk at Pilgrimage, a Liberal/Feminist Mormon Women's Gathering at Alta Lodge, in Utah, June 2011. Walking with the topic was a wonderful gift.

THE THEME OF WHOLENESS, and what that might mean, has woven through my life. Three areas of reflection on the topic have been particularly fruitful: holding and imagining patterns of wholeness; patterns of wholeness in the Scriptures; and patterns of wholeness in the world.

Images of Wholeness

I believe each of us can play a role in creating and increasing wholeness, and holding images of wholeness is one place to start. The first image comes from my own practice as I seek to hear and know the wholeness in myself. Quakers sometimes use the term "grounding" to refer to a spiritual sense of rootedness. The term alludes to an intangible experience of feeling your Spirit anchored deep within the earth, or deep within the Divine. When I sit in worship by myself, in whatever location, it often starts with attention to the image of being deeply rooted. This is a metaphorical practice of feeling my own roots go through the earth and feeling them extend and reach. Holding this image gives me a personal sense of keeping my center of gravity low enough so I won't topple over or get stuck in my head.

The second image comes from a time when we were living in West Virginia. We were members of the Charleston Friends Meeting, and I was asked to be clerk. In a Quaker meeting the clerk of the meeting is the administrative head, responsible for listening for the spiritual sense of the business meetings. It was a small meeting, with ten to fifteen people on a Sunday. As clerk, I felt some responsibility for making an effort to deepen worship, and the image which came to mind was of a maypole of light in the center of the room. Each Sunday as we settled into worship, I would imagine the light pillar in the center of the room, and then take strands of light and wrap them one at a time around each person in the room until I'd gone all the way around the circle. I felt the image was a way of holding up the wholeness we could be as a meeting gathered in worship.

The third image comes from a time when I had made a set of prayer beads I used while sitting in prayer in the mornings. There were sixteen beads — four large ones, each separated from the others by three small ones. I assigned people and responsibilities to the small beads, and for each of the large ones I held the earth, imagining the iconic view of the blue green globe in space.

Queries:

How might you need or want to imagine and hold a sense of wholeness in your own life and in the world around you?

How do you hold the wholeness and health of the earth?

Images of Wholeness in the Bible

While many scriptures carry invitations to wholeness, the Bible is the tradition I know best. I want to explore three different images: the parable of the Good Samaritan, the Law of Moses, and the story of Job.

The Good Samaritan

In the parable of the Good Samaritan, Jesus provides a hint of how we may need to act as individuals to fully embrace and create wholeness in the world. This story is often presented as a moral code, a guide for how we should behave to those in need. Ivan Illich, in *The Rivers North of the Future*,[1] offers a somewhat different interpretation. Jesus's message over and over again is about the importance of being present to the uniqueness of each individual. In this parable the Samaritan feels called, across ethnic lines, to help another. His pity and concern is a gift from God. When we read this story as an

---

1 David Cayley, *The Rivers North of the Future: The Testament of Ivan Illich* (Toronto: Anansi Press, 2005).

invitation to listen for when God is calling us to the person in the ditch, or in need, it may be a more welcome invitation than believing it is our job to help everyone in need. Illich suggests the story offers an invitation to listen for when our hearts are moved to pity and love, and to be open to the experience of meeting that of God in another across racial, ethnic, class and other boundaries in those moments. In our openness to listening and responding when so moved, we play our part in building and embracing wholeness in the world.

The Law of Moses

The Book of Deuteronomy chapter 2 speaks to a different kind of wholeness, offering a vision of the social contracts needed among human beings to live together in peace. The rules are quite interesting, and I'm just going to highlight a few. From Deuteronomy 15:1–2, 4:

> At the end of every seventh year you shall make a remission of debts. This is how the remission shall be made: everyone who holds a pledge shall remit the pledge of anyone indebted to him. He shall not press a fellow-countryman for repayment, for the Lord's year of remission has been declared. . . . There will never be any poor among you if only you obey the Lord your God by carefully keeping these commandments which I lay upon you this day.

Here the authors speak to the importance of forgiving debt, with the rule that every seven years there is a blanket forgiveness for all debtors.

Deuteronomy 23:15–16 speaks[2] to the importance of not returning fugitive slaves and not oppressing the slaves who live among them. "You shall not surrender to his master a slave who has taken refuge with you. Let him stay with you anywhere he chooses in any one of your settlements, wherever suits him best; you shall not force him." Later in the same chapter the Israelites are told they are not to charge interest to their brother Israelites, although they can charge foreigners interest. "You shall not charge interest on anything you lend to a fellow-countryman, money or food or anything else on which interest can be charged. You may charge interest on a loan to a foreigner but not on a loan to a fellow-countryman, for then the Lord your God will bless you in all you undertake in the land which you are

---

2 All translations are from the New English Translation, unless otherwise indicated.

entering to occupy." This is a particularly interesting rule to consider today when interest is expected for so many transactions. In the next chapter there is more on the theme of loans, and the Israelites are given detailed guidelines for when they provide a secured loan to another Israelite. They are to wait patiently to receive the security, without going into the home of the debtor. If the person receiving the loan is poor, they are not to keep the pledged item overnight. "When you make a loan to another man, do not enter his house to take a pledge from him. Wait outside, and the man whose creditor you are shall bring the pledge out to you. If he is a poor man, you shall not sleep in the cloak he has pledged. Give it back to him at sunset so that he may sleep in it and bless you; then it will be counted to your credit in the sight of the Lord your God."[3] All of these detailed rules can be seen as excessive nitpicking and arcane minutiae, but they can also be seen as guidelines to create a more just society; as the next step in limiting oppression of others.

Job

The third image I want to share from the scriptures is from the Book of Job. I am fascinated by the Book of Job, and am particularly moved by the poetry given to God when Job finally gets a response to his complaints. Using the New English Bible, I want to share a bit of the poetry. Remember, Job has lost all of his possessions and his children, and eventually his entire body is covered with sores. His friends have come to comfort him, and in their desire to comfort they keep asking what he did to deserve this punishment, since God is just and it could only happen if he deserved it. In the face of those challenges, Job continues to maintain his innocence, and to call on God to explain. And finally God responds: Who do you think you are! "Who is this whose ignorant words cloud my design in darkness? Brace yourself and stand up like a man; I will ask questions, and you shall answer. Where were you when I laid the earth's foundations?" "In all your life have you ever called up the dawn or shown the morning its place?" "Have you descended to the springs of the sea or walked in the unfathomable deep?" "Do you know when the mountain goats are born or attend the wild doe when she is in labour?"[4] These verses

3 Deuteronomy 23:10–14.
4 Job 38:2–4, 38:11, 38:16, 39:1.

speak to the wholeness of creation, and challenge Job — and us — to be more humble about what we think we understand about how the world works.

Queries:

What are the detailed guidelines we need today, at the individual level?

How should each of us behave to others so as to create a more whole community?

Images of Wholeness in the World

The final theme area I want to talk about is images of wholeness in the world. I have three examples: permaculture, the L'Arche communities, and wolves.

Permaculture

I first heard about permaculture in 1993, when I met Rosemary Morrow in Vietnam. Rosemary was working for the Australian Quaker Service, and she was working with rural Vietnamese communities to change their approach to gardening. I remember her saying, "Everybody gardens." And then she explained how the birds, worms, ants, and all other living things can be used to enhance the fertility of our food system if we think carefully and pay attention to the actions and needs of all the other players in the system. I didn't really understand what she meant, and it took another seventeen years for me to start looking in to permaculture. I started by reading *Gaia's Garden*, by Toby Hemenway, and I was hooked. As Hemenway describes it:

> The order of a conventional row-crop garden is the order of the machine. This regimentation invites us to view plants as mechanical food factories. We fuel them with fertilizer, service them with rakes and hoes, and measure their production in bushels, bins and tons. We view the plants as part of our dominion. In a guild, we are but one living being among many others; and like all the other animals enfolded by this community, we nurture and are nurtured by an almost-wild place. We prune and cull, as do the deer and mice. The fruit we leave does not rot on the ground to breed disease; it is gladly devoured by our many companions. We turn over a bit of soil, and the worms turn over yet more. We participate rather than rule. With

guilds, we can begin to shed the mantle of command and return to nature the many responsibilities we have unnecessarily assumed.[5]

Permaculture practitioners are looking for ways to mimic healthy ecosystems in our systems of food production, to learn from nature what plants work together and how we better fit our needs into functioning ecosystems. Guilds are the name given to a group of plants which become more than the sum of the parts when they are planted together, providing mutual support and enrichment. While we need to change our eating habits to better take advantage of the strengths of permaculture, decreasing consumption of grain and legumes, the trade-off of having gardens get stronger and more productive with time might be worth it. In addition, we get to learn to better understand the relationships in a healthy ecosystem. What an opportunity to enhance and embrace wholeness in the world!

L'Arche

One of the most striking examples I have seen of wholeness in the world are the L'Arche communities. First founded in France in 1964, these communities "bear witness to the reality that persons with intellectual disabilities possess inherent qualities of welcome, wonderment, spirituality and friendship." I first ran across these communities in the writings of Henri Nouwen, who wrote movingly of his experiences living in the Daybreak community outside of Toronto, Canada. Three of the key tenets of the L'Arche communities include the following:

> People with intellectual disabilities are at the heart of L'Arche. They're not clients, patients or recipients of services, but rather they are friends, teachers and companions.
> People without intellectual disabilities grow through their encounters in L'Arche. Through daily acts of care, trust and friendship, they develop into ambassadors of compassion and leaders of social change and the common good.
> A divided society is mended through inclusivity where people with many differences — socio-economic status, race, religion, and intellectual capacity — live and work together.[6]

5 Toby Hemenway, *Gaia's Garden* (White River Junction: Chelsea Green, 2009), p. 207.
6 https://www.larcheusa.org/learn/ (Accessed 10/26/2017)

This is a very different approach, seeking to live out the act of honoring and meeting that of God in another human being on a daily basis in an environment of love and respect for those with disabilities. Assistants play an important role in the communities, serving the core residents. Heather Bixler shared her reflections from her time in one of the L'Arche communities: "[Names], along with other core members in our house, are born counter-cultural. Their bodies and minds don't fit neatly into the mainstream understanding of what it means to be a person of worth. But through their daily acts of love and acceptance, my housemates have become my guides, pointing me towards the joy and promise of the Kingdom."[7] These communities are living experiments of how to live together with a deep concern for giving and receiving love. They stand as an example and a challenge to all of us.

Wolves

When I think about wholeness in the natural world, for some years I've been following a thread of wolves. It started some years ago when I read *Wolf Totem*, by Jiang Rong, in translation from the Chinese. In this story a teenage Han Chinese boy is sent to Mongolia during the Cultural Revolution. There he learns about the system and the way of life of the Mongolian herders from a Mongolian elder. He also watches the slaughter of the wolves by the Chinese, and with the slaughter comes the destruction of the grassland ecosystem. The reverse of the story has been demonstrated in Yellowstone National Park, with the reintroduction of wolves in 2001. The wolves had all been killed in the 1930s, but with a growing understanding of the importance of key predator species for the health of an ecosystem, they were brought back in 2001. Since then the park has gone from one beaver colony to nine, and springs are flowing that had not flowed for decades.[8] Piecing together the chain of events, biologists found elk do not graze on willows on open riverbanks when there are wolves; instead, they seek less exposed places to graze. This allows young willows to become available as food for beavers. This is just one example, but encourages us to reflect deeply on what wholeness in an ecosystem might look like.

---

7 https://www.larcheusa.org/2010/10/the-bigger-picture/ (Accessed 10/26/2017)
8 Information gleaned from the National Science Foundation's website, https://www.nsf.gov/discoveries/disc_summ.jsp?cntn_id=126853 (Accessed 10/26/17)

Queries:

How do we give and receive love across differences of all kinds?

How do you engage with natural resources under your care and control?

The Garden of Eden

The final image I want to bring up is the Garden of Eden. This is a foundational myth in western civilization, held by the three main monotheistic traditions. In this story we begin with a man and a woman living in a beautiful garden full of plants and animals. They fed themselves from the plants in the garden. They watched the animals and plants, learning by watching all the different ways the plants and animals worked together to make the garden fruitful and beautiful. They ate different fruits, nuts, greens and other plants. Maybe they ate eggs and meat — the story is vague on this point. What they didn't eat was the fruit of the tree in the center of the garden — the tree of knowledge of good and evil. God told them to avoid the tree, saying if they ate it, they would surely die. One day a serpent in the garden approached the woman. To paraphrase the story, the serpent says, "Woman, have you seen the fragrant and beautiful fruit on the big tree in the center of the garden?"

"Oh yes, but if we eat it we will die," she replied.

"Oh, woman," said the serpent, "that is only a story. The fruit of the tree will make you wise, like the Gods, knowing good and evil. You won't die. Come, look at how ripe the fruit is."

The woman looked again at the fruit, at how succulent it looked, and also thought about the wisdom which would come from eating the fruit, and finally decided to eat it. She ate a piece of fruit and then took it to the man to share, and he also ate. Their eyes were opened. All around them they saw new potential. Previously their days had been filled with laughter, games, exploration and observation as they watched and learned from the plants and animals. Now they could see all the ways the garden could be improved, starting with getting themselves some clothes. When God came to join them in the evening in the cool of the garden, they hid. When God called to them — "Man, woman, where are you?" The man replied "Lord, we have hidden from you to hide our nakedness."

With that statement, the man revealed their eyes had been opened; they now judged things as bad which they had previously accepted without question. They also decided they needed some protection from the world — clothes — a barrier to put between them and the rest of life. God sent them out of the garden and cursed the serpent to go forever on its belly. For the man and the woman, the promise was now they would till the ground in sorrow and give birth in pain for all of their days. With the eating of the fruit, this story has shaped western civilization. It provided a foundational myth of how man and woman have "fallen" and all the brokenness of the human structures in the world around us inevitably grow out of the fall. It also carries in it the idea we know good and evil, having eaten of the tree.

Through the centuries the story has been told as a factual account of historic events, as a true myth, and many gradations in between. My understanding, following recent authors such as Daniel Quinn,[9] is to interpret the story as a clash of civilizations at the dawn of agriculture. Hunter-gatherers lived (and still live) in a garden they know intimately; they have numerous uses for each animal and plant, seasons of availability, taste, and relationships. While the argument over the time budgets of hunter-gatherers are extensive, the most recent evidence suggests their work load was less and their health was better than generations of agriculturalists.[10]

I pray that we can walk more fully in ways that embrace the wholeness which is, and create more opportunities for wholeness in the world around us.

Queries

How do you hold the wholeness and health of the earth?

Where have you experienced your own wholeness?

---

9 Daniel Quinn, *Ishmael* (New York: Bantam Books, 1992).

10 Marshall Sahlins, *Stone Age Economics* (Hawthorne, NY: Aldine Publishing Company, 1972).

CHAPTER 11

Exploring the Unwritten Rules of Waiting Worship

E NERGETIC VOICES, periods of quiet, and bursts of giggles kept erupting from the four groups spread around the room. It was a July morning in 2007, and we'd given the workshop participants the task of making lists of the unwritten rules of waiting worship. Peter Crysdale and I were co-leading a Friends General Conference (FGC) Gathering workshop on deepening worship and inviting vital ministry. Our hope for the participants, who all came seeking to deepen the worship of their meetings, was that they would leave with tools which could help them nurture their worship with love and joy.

We had asked the four small groups to make lists with the hope that participants would have a sense of what rules were more common across meetings and what rules were unique to their own meeting, and then together we could talk about how the rules supported — and got in the way — of the moving of the Spirit. The actual lists aren't important, but what they allowed was the exploration together of how our expectations and internalized sense of rules affect our experience of worship. We believed our approach was valuable after observing how workshop participants identified rules and then deeply considered how the rules influenced their expectations for and experience of worship.

The Unwritten Rules

For some years now I have walked with a concern for the spiritual health and vitality of the Religious Society of Friends. One of my early observations about the life of the Spirit among Friends was the importance of the quality of our corporate worship. To further reflect on what individuals can do to deepen worship, Peter Crysdale and I co-led two workshops at New England Yearly Meeting and two at the FGC Gathering, all focused on how we can deepen worship and nurture vital ministry. In considering the quality of our worship, we came back again and again to the expectations we bring, both the positives (what we expect will happen) and the negatives (what we expect will not happen). Those expectations are what I've come to call the unwritten rules. In walking with expectations or unwritten rules, I've come to three groupings — container, content, and core. Container rules address the context and environment of our worship — things like the room, the time, entry and exit procedures. Content rules govern the form and content of the ministry during worship — things like the type of messages, spacing, and delivery. Core rules are at the heart of Quakerism, and they bring us back to the Presence and encourage our faithful obedience.

The next time I did this exercise on unwritten rules was in 2013, on a cold February night in the meeting house at the Woolman Hill Conference Center. This time we did it in one large group, as an introductory activity for a weekend workshop devoted to the topic. Kathleen Wooten and I were co-leading the workshop for a joint program sponsored by New England Yearly Meeting Ministry and Counsel, Woolman Hill Quaker Conference Center, and the Quaker Studies Program of Salem Quarterly Meeting. We each wrote a rule or two on index cards, placed them in a basket, and passed the basket around. Everyone took a card and read the rule on it. We all identified rules about timing, messages, or not talking too long.

While the FGC workshop had used only that exercise, this time we could go further. The next day, gathered by the wood stove in the dining room of the conference center, we moved on to experiments about changing the rules. For these experiments we had considered a number of different ways to test whether we could find a centered worshipful space through a range of containers and contents. We experimented with three "rules" about the worship container (chairs in a circle facing outward, all standing, and chairs in rows of four like on a train) and three rules about the form of ministry (ten words or less, no words, and only in song). Later that year when I repeated the workshop for Vassalboro Quarterly Meeting with Honor Woodrow, we added additional container options of kneeling in a circle and sitting in pairs. In both workshops, we drew the new "rules" at random after writing them on slips of paper, and then spent ten minutes in worship, using the new rule.

At Woolman Hill, the first rule we drew was to set the chairs in rows of four, with an aisle down the center. We called them "train chairs." We sat in those chairs in worship for ten minutes. The rows of chairs faced the northern window, looking out over the field with the dark wooden beams over head. We could feel the worshipers beside us, and to some extent in front and behind. The strangeness of the linear orientation, and the absence of someone looking back at us challenged the group. Messages questioned who or what we faced. We also held the deeper Spirit in the strangeness. Some months later, we were gathered in Big Bird Lodge at Friends Camp in South China Maine. A spacious room, with some twenty to twenty-five of us gathered in a circle on a very damp and cold day, we drew the container rule of kneeling in a circle. We offered pillows to those who wanted them, encouraged people to sit or stay in their chairs if they needed to, and the rest of us knelt. This practice challenged us all with questions. What do we kneel before? How do we humble ourselves? What do we lose in a faith that has no current tradition of kneeling? For each of the experimental "rules," there was rich ministry, informed by the new rule, but also reaching beyond the rule.

A Closer Examination of Two Common Rules

In these workshops we've played with rules, experimented with different rules, and also taken the time to hold more deeply the usefulness and the limitations of some of the common rules. Two of the common content rules, which were identified by all of the workshops and groups, are "Thou shalt leave space between messages" and "Thou shalt not speak twice." Both of these rules can be useful, but can also limit the Spirit.

Space Between Messages

The importance of space between messages has been stated as fact, or as a rule, numerous times. One New England Friend expressed to me that it was just plain courtesy to leave space between messages. I have listened to discussions where there was general agreement that a three-minute space between messages is essential. And yet I have also experienced times in worship when the moving of the Spirit was smooth and easy and there was little space between messages. Some years ago I was traveling in the Pacific Northwest, visiting meetings. We had gathered on Saturday evening with people in Multnomah Meeting in Portland, Oregon, who had support committees, to worship with them and share experiences. Sitting in worship on Sunday morning, the Spirit felt rich and strong. My journal entry says, "Deep worship, powerful, grounded messages (Journal, July 2006)." And yet towards the end of worship, there were multiple messages right after each other, and I was moved to speak. I struggled with timing, not wanting to insert my voice into the fray. And yet my traveling companion, Eleanor Godway, a seasoned elder, had been encouraging me to trust the timing of the Spirit. So I spoke. And despite the limited space between messages, the worship was deep and powerful.

Some years later, on a visit to Wellesley Meeting in New England, I was also traveling with Eleanor as my companion. The Dalai Lama had spoken in the area the day before, and people had been deeply stirred by his visit. In the sun-filled room there were several messages drawing on the Dalai Lama's visit, with a number towards the end of worship. I was moved to speak. After the rise of worship someone from their Ministry and Counsel took me aside and gently said he'd been asked to let me know I'd spoken too soon after the previous message. I responded I was trying hard to be faithful to the timing of the Spirit, and not to impose my sense of rightness on the timing of the message. At a later point I learned the meeting had a dear elderly friend who was hard of hearing, and someone was transcribing messages for her during worship, so space between messages was important for the transcribing friend to catch up.

A friend from New England Yearly Meeting shared a story of his experience in the closing worship one year at the Friends General Conference Gathering. Hundreds of people were gathered in worship, and messages were coming thick and fast. Eventually someone stood to ask for silence. And into the silence a cell phone rang out. Jim's reflection was of imagining it was God, asking "Did we get disconnected — I thought we had such a good connection!"

In 2010 New England Yearly Meeting had an experiment in extended worship. More than a hundred friends gathered in Portland, Maine for a mid-year gathering for extended worship at a hotel.

Chairs were arranged in a rectangle in a low-ceilinged meeting room. We entered into waiting worship on Friday evening, spent time in waiting worship Saturday morning and Saturday evening, and again on Sunday morning. Throughout the worship there were many voices, and many experienced the worship as chaotic. There was little silence. Yet I heard new voices, people who would never speak at our annual gathering in August, who had the courage to put themselves into the community. The chaos led the planning group to ask us on Saturday evening to center in worship and not to speak. I sat on the floor against a wall and grieved. It felt to me as if the rawness of the worship was scaring people, making us uncomfortable, and rather than riding through it, we had shut down the chaos.

Only Speak Once

Another common rule in worship is we should only speak once. In the context of worship sharing (see glossary), this rule is often made explicit, and speaking more than once also tends to be frowned on in waiting worship. Yet again, there are times in different meetings where I have experienced people speaking twice where it felt in the Spirit. Daphne Bye accompanied me on a visit to Dover Monthly Meeting on a late spring weekend, and while the vocal ministry was frequent, I had a clear sense of Spirit moving. One older friend, a well-respected elder, spoke early in worship, and then rose and spoke again towards the end.

In August 2013 in the Sunday morning worship of New England Yearly Meeting annual sessions, one of the pastors spoke twice. We were worshipping in a large, open round room, with folding chairs curved to the sides of the platform in the front. The children had left, the teens were no longer off to the side, and the adults were centering in worship following a keynote address which had included threads about language. The pastor spoke once and sat back down, then rose to speak again following another message. The person carrying the microphone looked long and hard, but the pastor nodded, and was given the microphone. In the message, s/he expressed a sense of not being fully faithful to the message the first time, and a need to share all that had been given. While I was not able to connect the two messages, I was moved by a sense of vitality and faithfulness in the ministry.

Core Rules

In Isaac Penington's 1660 essay "The Authority which Christ Excluded out of his Church," he addresses the question of chaos in worship, and hints at what he considers the core rules.

> When the Spirit moves in any one to speak, the same Spirit moves in the other to be subject and give way: and so every one keeping to his own measure in the Spirit, here can be no disorder, but true subjection of every spirit; and where this is wanting, it cannot be supplied by any outward rule or order set up in the church by common consent: for that is fleshly, and lets in the flesh, and destroys the true order, rule, and subjection.[1]

When the Body is not listening to the Spirit, we need to pray for listening. Creating outward rules distracts from the listening, curtailing the falling short and mistakes which can be an important part of the learning process.

For me, this question is at the core of Quaker worship. We come to worship seeking to listen to, and be obedient to, the Spirit. To further nurture the capacity to hear, we must practice the listening in our own lives on a daily basis.

Teaching and Learning the Rules

One of the challenges of these unwritten rules is how they are taught to new people. In my own meeting, Hartford, Connecticut, I was sitting in worship, and noticed a young woman nearby. I had not seen her in worship before. This particular day, unusually, I had slipped in a bit late and had chosen to sit at the back of the room near the door. Settling into worship, the young woman spoke, sharing a scripture and language of our Heavenly Father being generous and loving. Ten to fifteen minutes later she spoke again, in a similar vein. After another ten or fifteen minutes, maybe forty minutes into meeting, she stood and slipped out the back door. I rose and slipped out after her. She said she had to be somewhere, but was open to sitting for a few minutes. I told her I hoped she'd be back, I could feel the Spirit moving and affirmed her spiritual journey. She mentioned how wonderful

---

1 Isaac Penington, *The Works of Isaac Penington: A Minister of the Gospel in the Society of Friends*, Vol. 1 (Glenside, PA: Quaker Heritage Press, 1995) p. 382.

she found the open space. I shared my hope she would return, and a gentle note that we generally only find that Spirit moves us to speak once in worship. I regretted saying anything about the speaking twice — there would have been time later. After worship, multiple people came up to me to thank me for following the young woman out, and several explicitly expressed their concerns that she needed to be eldered for speaking twice. I haven't seen this young woman return. Perhaps she will at some point, but we weren't particularly welcoming, and my sharing of her "rule violation" may easily have driven her away.

These stories speak to the challenge of how we learn Quaker worship. Is it something one intuitively gets? My experience is Quaker worship, and particularly waiting worship, is a skill we are building both individually and corporately. The skill is fundamentally about listening to, and being obedient to, the Spirit, which for me are the core rules. I try to practice listening and obedience on a daily basis, and I fall short all the time. I am often not quite on the right channel — sometimes it feels like my dial is just a little bit off. When we gather in worship with others, we're also practicing tuning. Sometimes the learning process may involve allowing ourselves and others to get it wrong. When we think someone else got it wrong, it requires careful listening to discern whether it is our place to tell them they misheard, or to invite them to hold the question of whether they misheard, or perhaps we are to hold them in love and have faith that the Spirit, the Inward Teacher, is also at work in their life.

As I have walked with the three groupings of rules, my experience is we often substitute container and content rules when we have not spent time as a community with the core rules. Deep and rich worship could be nurtured by a discussion of what we each see as the core rules of Quaker worship, and what we each experience and are listening for as we sit together in the silence. Container and content rules may create something which looks very similar to what we expect when we're living with the core rules. If we don't have the core, it can be tempting to substitute container and content rules to get us the form we might get if we were listening deeply. Sometimes it works. But unless we're clear the core is where the worship has to come from, we may not understand the usefulness and limitations of the container and content rules, and the container and content rules can find a life of their own.

Queries

When are we trying to make the worship look right, rather than waiting on the Spirit and seeing what emerges?

How do we approach worship in a spirit of openness to the Spirit moving beneath the words, ready to take on a gentle stream or Niagara Falls, as the Spirit moves?

How do we listen deeply for the guidance of the Spirit when the worshiping community has a diversity of needs?

CHAPTER 12

The Lies I Live

A S AN INCOMING STUDENT to the Honors Program at Brigham Young University in 1980, I was assigned an essay by Aleksandr Solzhenitsyn. A key phrase stuck in my mind I have carried since then — something about the blindness of superiority.[1] It was in reading Solzhenitysn's essay that I remember first considering the belief in Western superiority as something other than true. Norbert Elias, writing about civilization in 1930s Germany, started with an observation: the construct of civilization is the self-concept of the west. He notes the term is used to characterize the behaviors, technology and social structures of the western world seen to set the western world apart as better than traditional societies. In reading Elias's *The Civilizing Process*, two ideas were transformational: civilization is the self-concept of the west, and civilization is the increasing control of instinct and affect. I have personally struggled with the terms civilized, or civilization, particularly as used during the colonial era, since they were virtually always a comparison between a western person or group and a non-western, native or aboriginal person or group. The western culture was perceived as more civilized, and the non-western person or thing was perceived as less civilized. By this definition of civilized, someone who was non-western, who lived by different values, was uncivilized. Since manners are a key element of what is judged when making the determination of whether someone is "civilized," the west has judged others with a superficially objective standard by how civilized they are, while in reality the question being asked is, "How different are they from me?" If they're different, the implication is they're less civilized.

For years I've walked with the question of what is culture and what is truth. Another way I've framed the question is how do I see more fully the seeds of war in my life. "Seeds of war" is the language

---

1 "A World Split Apart," by Alexander Solzhenitsyn, delivered at Harvard University 8 June 1978, available online at http://www.americanrhetoric.com/speeches/ alexandersolzhenitsynharvard.htm (Accessed 11/1/2017).

John Woolman uses to refer to the pieces of our daily lives which carry inequity and injustice. These are the seeds of war. It's the goods or services we use in our lives which involved oppression somewhere in the production or supply system that brought them to us. When I first read John Woolman's journal and his essay, "A Plea for the Poor,[2] in the early 2000s, I was struck by his reflections and started carrying the question of where there might be seeds of war in my life. While I'd been asking these questions for a long time, clarity started to come when I was introduced to the concept of decolonization in 2013.

Encountering Decolonization

The title was "Decolonizing HIV research using arts-based methods," and it jumped at me from the pages of poster titles in the conference book. My morning (or evening) ritual at the American Public Health Association's annual meeting was to scan the titles of upcoming posters and write down the numbers of those I really want to see, so I can find them among the hundreds of posters in each session. Intrigued by the title, I decided to talk with the authors to try to understand what they were talking about. In the cavernous Boston convention center, one of the authors was standing at the poster near the end of the row. I shared how intrigued I was by their title and asked her to tell me about their work. Sarah Flicker, from Toronto, shared their starting point — colonized peoples, whether in southern Africa or rural Canada, are at increased risk of HIV. There is an internalization of the oppressor's devaluation, which leaves colonized peoples acting in ways that increase their own risk. The research team was working with teens in South Africa and First Nations teens in Canada, using art to help the youth examine their sense of identity, and the internalized oppression which left them devaluing their own self-worth. The poster grabbed me at a very visceral level, and I started walking with this understanding of colonization and decolonization.[3]

Being grounded in the academic system, I started with a search on decolonization in the Yale library system. Title after title came up on

2 John Woolman, *The Journal and Major Essays of John Woolman*, edited by Phillips P. Moulton (Richmond, IN: Friends United Press, 1989).

3 To be clear, by colonization I mean the imposition of a value system and world view on the less powerful by the more powerful. When colonization is really successful the colonized internalize the value system and perpetuate the devaluation themselves.

my screen, showing a field of scholarship I had never heard of. I found a book by Susan Najita entitled *Decolonizing Cultures in the Pacific*, which I ordered and read as a starting point.[4] It is a literary analysis of how authors from the Pacific Islands since the 1970s have struggled with the burden of colonization, and how native authors have incorporated colonization themes into their books. Najita's book was important in opening my eyes, as were several of the books she analyzed.

The first book which arrived via interlibrary loan was *The Leaves of the Banyan Tree*, by Albert Wendt, set in Samoa. As I read, I found it interesting to watch my emotional reaction to the book. The story starts with a young man in his village who went to a mission school and now wants all the things of the foreigners. The first chapter sets up beautifully the aching of desire and longing for material goods that makes it difficult for the colonized to reject the colonizers. As I read, I had a deep visceral foreboding, which made it hard to continue reading. My emotional apprehension centered around a gut response to how this story has played out so many other times. Wendt tells a story of the insidiousness of the drive to power and the seductiveness of using other people to achieve one's own ends. *Leaves of the Banyan Tree* is also about the seductiveness of the life of *papalagi* (foreigners), and the willingness of native peoples to accept the ethics and standards of foreigners. At one point early in the novel, an older woman tells her grandson the *papalagi* brought Christianity and then stopped practicing it, as she names the disjunction between Jesus's teachings and the values of accumulation, manipulation, and using other people for one's own ends, that were rampant among the foreign colonizers. The ending involves a sense of the right outcome for the good of the people and the tribe, achieved by blackmailing a corrupt attorney. In essence, the ethics and legal structures of the *papalagi* can stand in the way of the right thing being done for the community and the land.

Native peoples across the globe are taking on the work of decolonization — identifying and stepping away from the beliefs and value system of the colonizers. Native peoples have been using the term decolonization to refer to the process of reclaiming their own value

---

4 Susan Najita, *Decolonizing Cultures in the Pacific: Reading History and Trauma in Contemporary Fiction* (New York: Taylor and Francis, 2006).

system and attending to when their default behaviors arise from the value system of the colonizers. As a descendent of the historical colonizers, I feel compelled to honor and respect the language native peoples are using for their work. As they do this important work, there is a parallel work of decolonization I need to pick up, as a descendant of the traditional oppressors. The work is not the same, and it is both essential and insufficient to focus on being allies of the oppressed.

The concept of colonization is most often applied to invading bacteria, peoples and plants, and in all these contexts refers to the establishment of a viable presence, a colony. Colony is the noun, while colonization refers to the process whereby a new organism first shows up and then lives and reproduces. I'm using the term in a slightly different way, to refer to the process by which cultural values and ideas are first presented and then adopted and internalized. For three years I walked with the question, "What is the decolonization I need?" I wrestled with it, talked with friends and strangers about decolonization over and over, seeking to identify and name the fundamental values and beliefs at the root of the misalignment between human needs, human systems, and the health of the planetary system. Early in my walk with decolonization a friend asked what would be lost if I found some language other than decolonization, since the concept of decolonization was very challenging for many of the people I've talked with. I realized using a different language would be stepping away from the language native peoples are using, and allowing the white people to once again control the language for the sake of their own comfort. The use of the term also forces me to own the historical colonization, and the negative impacts of colonization. As I walked, four areas kept coming back: relationship with the natural world, religious beliefs, economic systems, and social structures.

Summer 2015: Synthesizing Threads Through Travel

Drinking tea and eating scones smothered in butter, jam and whipped cream, I sit in a café outside Caernarfon Castle in North Wales, resting after walking around the castle and village for much of the day. This is the location where the English claimed the title of Prince of Wales in 1283, and where the current Prince of Wales was crowned in 1969. I sit at a booth by the window, watching visitors go in and out of the castle. When I wandered through the castle earlier, I was struck by how all the displays were written from a point of view of Great Britain rather than a Welsh point of view. Upon leaving, I ask the ticket collector what he thinks the Welsh version of the story would be. He agrees the displays represent a British/United Kingdom perspective. Later, when I share my reflections with the host of my Airbnb, he tells me that as a teenager, when the Prince of Wales was crowned, some of his friends were locked up during the celebrations because the local police were concerned they would make a ruckus. The next day I notice the low flying Royal Air Force training flights buzzing the hills and valleys, and experience a sense of the colonial yoke in Wales today.

Three weeks after my time in Wales I'm in Chefchaouen, Morocco, sitting under a fig tree, with my back against a rough stone wall. The tour group of American teachers I was with walked through the city in the morning, trekking over rough stone pebbles embedded in concrete in narrow lanes and alleys. It's the twenty-eighth day of Ramadan, and at 9:30 a.m. the alleys are almost deserted. Chefchaouen is known as a blue city, with walls throughout painted a pale blue/lavender color, a custom attributed to the founders, Jewish refugees from the Spanish Inquisition in 1471. The city is set on a hillside, and we walk up from our guest house to the last lane of houses, just before the upper city wall. From there we go down, and soon make it to a beautiful tree-filled ravine. Multiple stone staircases make paths to different levels of the river. Two beautiful washing shelters provide washing basins with scrubbing boards. I wonder what it would be like to do laundry here with friends, scrubbing and talking together. On each side of the river there's a concrete shelter with an ingenious washing platform. There are multiple concrete basins with attached corrugated washboards, and water from the river flows down a channel in the middle of the platform. There are basins for clothes and soap, together with flowing water to rinse. How different the act of doing laundry must be when it's a group activity. I think back to a visit to Malawi some years ago, where I kept hearing how lazy the men in the villages were, and how they were always sitting around playing bao.[5] At the time, I had a chance to visit a village, where

5 Bao is a game of stones or markers that are moved through rows of bins in a board or holes in the ground.

people from several communities had gathered to meet with the staff of the NGO I was with, and to talk to a fairly large group of men and women. When we asked the men about the bao games, they said playing the game was a time for them to talk. They asked each other questions about the weather, whether they thought there was going to be a drought, whether there was someone who needed help with their fields, whether they should plant extra fields, when it was a good time to plant. What to westerners and city people looked like a waste of time was actually a key social technology, which created space for communication and corporate decision-making. We also asked the women about the times they got together to talk, and they reported doing so often, sometimes in prayer meetings, sometimes informally. They regularly gathered to think about the well-being of others in the community.

The absence of such spaces in many "developed" countries and the cities of lower and middle income countries makes it difficult for people from those places to fully understand the importance and value of these shared public spaces and seemingly recreational activities.

Towards the end of the Morocco trip, in conversation with others, I gave voice to four specific concerns about colonization, centered on the natural world, scripture, and metrics of value and hierarchy. I first wrote them as positive statements of the changes I wanted to work toward, in myself and in the world around me, and then with time realized I'd have to start by naming and acknowledging the lies I live. Once I have owned the lies, I hope it will be possible for me to change, to ground my life in the truths that are the reverse of the lies.

Lie #1: Humans are separate from the natural world

Our lives are constructed for more and more separation, with most activities taking place behind human-constructed walls.[6] The global economy is dependent on the right/ability to commodify natural

6 Many people have written of this separation. A few texts that have been influential for me: Morris Berman, *Coming to our Senses* (New York: Simon & Schuster, 1989); Gerry Mander, *In the Absence of the Sacred: The Failure of Technology and the Survival of the Indian Nations* (San Francisco: Sierra Club Books, 1991); David Cayley, *The Rivers North of the Future: The Testament of Ivan Illich* (Toronto: House of Anansi Press, 2005).

resources and people, and to treat them as interchangeable widgets. The lumber extracted through illegal logging from a tropical forest in the Congo Basin is treated the same as the lumber from a sustainably managed tropical forest in Brazil. We are told lumber is a resource, wasted if not actively contributing to human commerce and serving human needs. Trees are reduced to a raw material, rather than a living part of a complex system of planetary air-purification that animals, humans and the planet depend on for health.[7]

Lie #2: We can find literal/factual truth in scriptures

The story of the Garden of Eden in Genesis, where God chases Adam and Eve out of the garden, sentencing them to a life of pain and toil, earning their bread with the sweat of their brow, is foundational to Lie #1, as is the place in Genesis where humans are given dominion or stewardship over the natural world. Those who accept these scriptural traditions, though particularly Christians, often behave as if selective elements of this story are factually true — claiming a God-given right and responsibility to be stewards of the planetary ecosystem. The book of Genesis carries the transformative message that the land belongs to humans, rather than humans belonging to the land, a more common belief among native and indigenous peoples around the world. The conquest of Canaan in the Book of Joshua has been used to justify the deeply held belief that if God gives land to his chosen people, those so chosen have the right to kill, enslave or expel others. This is one of the foundational beliefs of the last four hundred years: colonization of the American, Asian and African continents rest on a perceived God-given primacy of believers, founded in a selective literal/factual interpretation of the first few books of the Bible.[8] The 2006 National Geographic *Concise History of the World: An Illustrated Timeline*, has a chapter on "The Birth of

---

7 There are many authors who have linked today's separation and commodification of natural resources with the emergence of the mechanistic world view that is now accepted as science. A couple that have been important for me: Gerry Mander, *In the Absence of the Sacred: The Failure of Technology and the Survival of the Indian Nations* (San Francisco: Sierra Club Books, 1991); John Ralston Saul, *On Equilibrium: Six Qualities of the New Humanism* (New York: Viking Press, 2001).

8 I avoid the language of Old and New Testament because it embodies the fallacy that Christianity replaced or supercedes Judaism.

Monotheism"[9] which assigns approximate dates to Biblical events such as Moses delivering the Israelites from Egypt (Exodus 13:17–22), despite there being no archaeological evidence to support the story of the Hebrew exodus from Egypt.[10] Marcus Borg, in *Reading the Bible Again for the First Time*,[11] writes of the importance of revising previous generations' interpretation of the Bible as a literal/factual historical account, without throwing away the amazing truth there is in the Bible. The presentation of particular Bible stories as "history" and justification for current actions and land law, is fundamentally problematic.

Lie #3: The only universal metric of value is money

We reduce everything to a dollar value, seeking to compare apples to apples. One of the things we lose in the monetary accounting is the ability to value human relationships and the gifts of time, care and love that nurture our souls. A graduate student from Bhutan shared with me her struggles with loneliness due to all the time she had alone while studying in the United States, in stark contrast to the network of relationships filling her days in Bhutan. She was blaming herself for not being strong enough to spend so much time alone, not able to see the epidemic of depression and loneliness around her. The global epidemic of depression is evidence of a deep rottenness in the global human culture. The inability to value relationships when there is no recognized system of value leaves people trapped. Every traditional society has had men's work and women's work. Ivan Illich, in *Gender*,[12] writes compellingly of what we have lost in seeing only the gender discrimination in the role separation. He notes the benefit of multiple systems of value and exchange — a system of gift or relationship values often practiced by women, and a system of financial valuation dominated more by men. Economic growth in the west has come by moving as much activity as possible from the gift system into the financial system.

9 *National Geographic Concise History of the World: An Illustrated Timeline*, edited by Neal Kagan (Washington D.C.: National Geographic Society, 2006).

10 Carol Meyers, *Exodus* (Cambridge: Cambridge University Press, 2005).

11 Marcus Borg, *Reading the Bible Again for the First Time* (New York: Harper Collins, 2009).

12 Ivan Illich, *Gender* (New York: Pantheon Books, 1982).

Lie #4: Hierarchy is the only functional structure for social organizations

Hierarchy, the ranking of the value of different human beings in terms of their functional value on a scale, will always lead to oppression, as someone has to be at the bottom. Bill Moyer reports hearing Lyndon Johnson say "If you can convince the lowest white man he's better than the best colored man, he won't notice you're picking his pocket."[13] A small dose of hierarchy, of being better than someone else, is addicting. The right to control the destiny of another, whether animal, vegetable or mineral, is similarly addicting. The feelings of unearned superiority can be hard to see past, and once experienced, there may be an unintended urge to grow the experience. Once humans on the path to complex societies began to justify hierarchy as progress — whether Asian, Assyrian, Aztec or western — it was hard to see the costs and downside of that hierarchy. While hierarchy is not needed for complex societies (remember the Iroquois Nation), it is needed for oppression and capitalism.

There is a fifth, overarching lie, that western civilization is the apex of human progress. Each of these lies has a parallel truth, and learning how to notice where I'm living from the lies and replace those behaviors by living the corresponding truths is my own work of decolonization. I am seeking my own praxis of decolonization, hoping to learn from the decolonization work of native peoples.

Towards a Praxis of Decolonization

In *Yakama Rising*, Michelle M. Jacob tells stories of the development of a decolonizing praxis by the Yakama community in central and eastern Washington.[14] The community had been working for years

13 "If you can convince the lowest white man he's better than the best colored man, he won't notice you're picking his pocket. Hell, give him somebody to look down on, and he'll empty his pockets for you." Lyndon Baines Johnson, to young staffer Bill Moyers in 1960, quoted in the Hightower Lowdown, volume 18 number 7, Aug 2016.

14 There is a schematic of challenges to cultural revitalization that includes three cascading elements: settler colonialism (restricted access to traditional foods), in combination with patriarchy (destructive gender norms; hierarchies of human / animal and human / nature are naturalized), feeding into white supremacy (omnipresence of western junk food system; continued erosion of traditional Yakama social and economic systems). Michelle M. Jacob, *Yakama Rising: Indigenous Cultural Revitalization, Activism and Healing* (Tucscon, AZ: University of Arizona Press, 2013).

with questions of decolonization and how best to nurture cultural knowledge, pride and heritage. One chapter tells of the Wapato Indian Club at a middle school, where kids learned and performed traditional dances. The advisor, the only Yakama counselor in the school district (in the early 1970s when the club began) described four key elements to her teaching process: (1) it must be fun, (2) students need to be respectful of the gifts of tradition and knowledge they are receiving, (3) students need to dedicate themselves to learning the dances, with a high standard of excellence, and (4) students must be high achievers and do a good job of performing so they know they did a good job and are proud of themselves. In reading these I was struck by the first element, fun, and the combination of fun with an emphasis on excellence. All of the chapters highlight the fundamental role of women in this work, with native women elders as culture bearers, and the importance of the complementary gender roles in the cultural heritage. I wonder what my decolonizing praxis is, and what the underlying principles are. What is the decolonizing praxis that I need as a white person with a dominant mix of Welsh and Scottish ancestry?

When I started walking with decolonization in 2013, holding questions of how I have been colonized, how I have helped to impose colonization on others, how I have worked on my own decolonization, and how I have encouraged and aided the steps towards decolonization of others, I went back to my journals. I started keeping a journal in December 1979 as a fifteen year old, when my parents gave me a journal for a Christmas present. My journaling has gone in cycles, with periods of very regular entries and then years with only a handful of entries. Over the course of eighteen months I transcribed all my journals into computer files. Through the journals I name several elements of my decolonizing praxis — reading, travel, hand sewing, gardening, and one that centers around my backyard — sitting in my backyard, and being in relationship with my backyard.

Some years ago I read Westley, Zimmerman and Patton's *Getting to Maybe: How the World is Changed*.[15] It is a book about social movements, describing how individuals were able to garner support and stimulate moderate to large scale social changes. I was frustrated at the end, and walked for several weeks with the book, trying to

15 Frances Westley, Brenda Zimmerman and Michael Quinn Patton, *Getting to Maybe: How the World is Changed* (Toronto: Random House Canada, 2006).

understand my discomfort. What eventually came up was the image of change as a wave, and how all the examples in the book were of people who caught a wave. What was missing was the process of how a wave is built. I connected that insight with a book I had read several years earlier for my Quaker women's book group. *Wide as the Waters*[16] is about the early English translations of the Bible. I had noticed a cycle in that book, where someone would stand up and say something heretical about the church or the Bible, they would be metaphorically or literally killed, and some years later, their perspective would be the norm. Wycliffe spoke of the importance of the separation of church and state, Tynsdale of the need for a vernacular Bible that anyone could read. Many of Wycliffe's followers were killed for heresy, although Wycliffe died of a stroke, and Tynsdale was convicted of heresy and burned. The separation of church and state unfolded over the hundred years following Wycliffe's death, and Tynsdale's vernacular translation of the Bible was accepted a year after his burning, and also is understood to make up over eighty percent of the King James translation of the Bible. I started thinking about the process of building a fifty-year wave, and holding the question, what are the long term changes we need? What waves need to be built to foster the decolonizing process? How do we speak today's heresy so it can become tomorrow's truth?

The Truths I Know

I can identify the converse of the lies, to name the underlying truths, but manifesting these truths in my daily life is daunting. The language of decolonization, and working to build my own practice of decolonization (a decolonizing praxis), is guiding my path forward.

Humans are an integral part of the natural world

When we live as if the natural world is "out there," something separate, something we can commodify, we threaten the health and functioning of the planetary ecosystem. Deborah Bird Rose, in *Report from a Wild Country: Ethics for Decolonization*,[17] shares the

---

16 Benson Bobrick, *Wide as the Waters* (New York: Simon & Schuster, 2001).

17 Deborah Bird Rose, *Reports from a Wild Country: Ethics for Decolonisation* (Sydney: UNSW Press, 2004).

perspective from an Aboriginal philosopher, Mary Graham. Mary identifies two basic precepts of the aboriginal world view: (1) The land is the law, and (2) You are not alone in the world. Both of these resonate for me. The land is the law. The health of the earth has to come first. This is the natural law, and in today's Western societies and education systems we don't learn about the laws inherent in the land and ecosystems. You are not alone in the world speaks to me at two levels. First is the sense that each human being shares the earth — the land, air and water — with other human beings, and it is important to consider the interests of other humans as we live in the land. Second is the reminder that there are other beings who are also on this land. Deborah Bird Rose shares the aboriginal sense of wild country as land which is exploited and abused by humans. Quiet land is land which is loved and cared for, for itself. This language challenges the western (and United States) priority of creating "wild" spaces untouched by humans — natural parks which exclude native peoples from their traditional lands, assuming humans can only degrade lands. If we are to live as a part, we need to be integrated, not separate. How do I live in relationship with quiet land?

Decolonizing Praxis

What does this mean for me? I'm trying to listen to my backyard. How do I build healthy soil? How do I attend to the plants that want to grow (some people call them weeds), and what can I learn about the physical space by listening?

Journal entry, November 2014

Falling leaves: The first that catches my eye after I settle myself on the bench, snuggly wrapped in a quilt against the freezing temperature, is a large maple leaf that swoops through the air, leaving behind its home tree. The next are two small maple leaves, falling as if twins, side by side, not quite plummeting, but definitely taking a straight and direct route to the ground. I sit with my back against a maple tree and watch more leaves. A large maple leaf, maybe six to eight inches across, spins slowly as it falls directly downward. With so many leaves on the ground it is easier to see the pair of cardinals on the fence line, and then the jay that lands in the mulberry tree. The mulberry seems to be the last to show green leaves in the spring and the last to lose green leaves in the fall. The mulberry leaves are still green; the maple leaves and trees are distinct in their yellow, the two large oak trees have red-brown leaves, and the two northern catalpa are more of a dirty red-brown. Sitting on the bench, a single leaf in the apple tree catches my eye, as it spins madly, almost frenetically, while all the other leaves around it are absolutely still. The spinning leaf is brown, while the leaves around it form a green audience. How can one leaf spin? What force is directing that spinning leaf?

It's a large city lot, almost a third of an acre, stretching deeply into the block — four houses border us on the side closest to the next cross street. The house sits at the front of the lot, with a paved parking area right behind and then the yard stretching back to the garage of the house through the block. In the spring and summer it's a vibrant green forest with houses visible but separate through the trees. There are two large oak trees at the northwest and northeast corners that turn rusty red-brown in the fall, and nine or ten maples of more than six inches in diameter that line the north and south property lines. And then the mulberries — there's a small one by the front driveway that covered the driveway with purple fruit the first year we were in the house. But the branches hung low over the driveway, and we haven't had any fruit since we pruned it. There's another big mulberry at the southeast corner of the pavement, where one end of the pulley clothesline is hooked. The big mulberry bowed low during the October snowstorm in 2011, full of leaves that caught and held the snow. One big branch came down, taking out our telephone line, but the rest of the tree bounced back. I notice from my vantage point farther back in the yard, sitting with my back against a maple, the top of the mulberry is still bent to the side, as if it remembers the weight of the snow that it carried. It's taken me a couple of years to notice the bend in the mulberry tree — lots of time sitting outside, noticing other things about the plants and other living things passing through the yard. Every day I sit outside with an open mind, I see something new. How can it be my nine years of living in the house bordering this space has only scratched the surface of the ecology and ecosystem? I think the squirrels eat the apples from the apple tree in the center of the yard, dividing a grassy area from the more wild space to the back. I haven't ever been home on the day each year the apples disappear from the branches, with many left on the ground with a few gnawed places on them. Soon those gnawed apples disappear also. Is it squirrels? Birds? A rat? Raccoon? Skunk? I'm just not sure. I suspect squirrels, but it may be a more complex story. There are other puzzles in the yard — the wild grape vines that tangle with the wild rose and pokeweed under the largest towering maple at the edge of the driveway. Where did it come from? Have there ever been grapes?

I hunger to know this small plot. To know where the mouse has its home, where the turkey really likes to hang out, what I can do to bring more songbirds to the back yard. To understand which plants are biennial, with different forms, and the uses of each. The final stanza from Sam Hamill's "A Lover's Quarrel" rings in my mind:

> I'd kiss a fish
> And love a stone
> And marry the winter rain
> If I could persuade this battered earth
> to let me make it home.[18]

All scriptures contain truth, and pursuit of factual truth in scriptures is a diversion from the deeper spiritual truths

While there may be portions of scriptures which are factual, it is virtually impossible to confirm what sections are factual given the time that has passed and the ways human communication and recording of these scriptures have likely altered the text. When we focus on finding fact we are missing the deeper truths at the core of all religious traditions. Scriptures around the world are evidence of the breakthrough of the spiritual into our lives. Literal interpretations can mask the deeper paradoxical truths at the core of all religious traditions.

Decolonizing Praxis

The Bible has been a part of my life since early childhood. I've read the scriptures with my family and by myself. As a child in the Mormon

18 Sam Hamill, *Destination Zero: Poems 1970–1995* (Fredonia, NY: White Pine Press, 1995), p. 7.

Church I was taught that the Bible is the word of God, as far as it is translated correctly. As a young adult I disengaged from the Bible as a spiritual text, and explored other scriptures, including texts such as the *Koran*, the *Tibetan Book of the Dead*, Confucius, Eknath Easwaran's translation of the *Bhagavad Gita*, and *The Gospel of Thomas*. I have long been fascinated by the writings we name holy, who names them holy, and how they come to be perceived that way. Early in my journey of living with a call to Quaker ministry I went back to the Bible, seeking to read it anew with the approach Robert Barclay, a seventeenth-century Quaker, emphasized, of reading it in the Spirit in which it was written.[19] This has continued to be my practice.

Journal entry, March 2014

Reading Hosea last night I was struck by 13:11: "I gave you a king in my anger, and in my fury took him away." My first reaction is to think back on the story in Samuel where the Israelites cry to Samuel to ask God to give them a king, so they can be like the other peoples around them. God tells Samuel the people are refusing to let God be their king, and he tells the people all the ways a king will abuse them. But they still want a king. God tells Samuel okay, I'll give them a king. And eventually the lineage of kings does lead to all the abuses and the heavy burden God had warned the people of.

As I read the Hebrew Bible this time I think I'm reading it and listening for what the stories and words tell us about the world views of the people at that time. When I think about God, the divine principle, I think about the ether, the space between the protons, neutrons and electrons. The amazing emptiness and spaciousness which pervades our beings. There are Quakers now who talk about being non-theist. To me that means embracing an understanding of God other than the white male. And yet I still like to use the word God, as a meme, a code for the universal principle I experience with the fire in my belly.

Going back to Hosea, he invites Israel to repent and return to God, swearing off their idols "What we have made with our own hands we will never again call gods; for in thee the faithless find a father's love." And God's response is "I will heal their apostasy; of my

19 Robert Barclay, *Apology for the True Christian Divinity*, first published in 1678 (Farmington, ME: Quaker Heritage Press edition, 2002).

own bounty will I love them; for my anger is turned away from them."

The thread I come back to is God's anger. There is a "modern" worldview, the peaceable kingdom world view, which seeks the absence of conflict. But what if anger and emotions are another kind of truth, a message like in the Pete Seeger song "Letter to Eve": "If you want to have great love, you've got to have great anger." What if violations of the universal divine principle create folds or wrinkles in the patterns of the universe, which are experienced somewhere in the system as pain or suffering?

As I write I notice the implicit assumption about the goal being to live a pain-free life. What if the goal instead is to understand that it is in part through our emotions we experience the world fully? How do I learn from my emotions rather than divorcing them as irrational, immature, or socially unacceptable? I read and listen as I read, seeking to feel the deep truths.

A healthy system of monetary exchange has to be balanced by an equally healthy system of gift and relationship exchanges

We need to strengthen the system of relationship exchange and reduce the role of monetary exchanges in our daily lives, and in how we meet fundamental human needs. The ability of a society to honor the value and importance of what used to be women's work, while also honoring the importance of removing the gender discrimination associated with such work, would be a dramatic step forward. At the very beginning of his book, *Plant Intelligence and the Imaginal Realm*,[20] Stephen Harrod Buhner tells of hearing Elisabeth Kübler-Ross share her story of why she does the work she does. Her story begins with a visit to one of the Nazi death camps, where she meets a young German (Jewish) woman, who had been spared the gas chamber when they couldn't make the door close behind her. The young woman shared her sense of what she'd learned from the Nazis. There is a little Hitler in each one of us, and if the little Hitler isn't

---

[20] Stephen Harrod Buhner, *Plant Intelligence and the Imaginal Realm* (Rochester, NY: Inner Traditions Bear and Company, 2014).

healed, the violence will never stop. I walked with the power of this woman's story, as told by Elisabeth Kübler-Ross, and come to the understanding that the financial economy feeds on and fosters the little Hitler. It is often our sense of inadequacy which leads to more and more consumption, as advertising plays on our insecurities. I wonder if a relationship or gift economy is the only thing that can heal the little Hitler.

Decolonizing Praxis

Where do I see the gift/relationship system most clearly? In rural communities in the United States and around the world.

I missed the turn off, but the unmarked road to the right was about where Google maps said I should turn to get to the Fremont County Golf Course. When we'd lived there thirty-five years before I'd never gone to the golf course. I turned off the four lane highway onto the side road. The parking lot was small, with some fifteen to twenty cars. Smaller than I expect. A minivan pulled up beside my rental car, and I recognized the passenger — "Teresa!" We hugged and said hi, both a little uncomfortable filling the space of thirty-five years since we last saw each other, and went in to the small boxy clubhouse.

This was the first high school reunion I'd even thought about attending, partly because I was going to be in the west (Phoenix) for a conference, and Phoenix, Arizona is close to Idaho when you live in Connecticut, and partly because I've been curious about the people I went to school with. It was a small crowd, some twenty-five people out of a class of just over one hundred. Shauna, the organizer, was disappointed with the turnout from the locals, naming some twenty others who lived within a couple of miles. Dinner was a delicious barbecue pork and baked potatoes (of course — St. Anthony, Idaho — the heart of potato country). I struggled with how to tell my story since high school in a way that would capture the nuances, knowing that my life looks exotic and exciting from the outside. I asked about the families — kids, grandkids, children with special needs, caregiving that has filled and enriched their lives. Shauna invited each of us to say a few words, where we've been, what we've done. My heart was pierced when one classmate said she felt like she hasn't done anything since high school, while she also told of raising six children and her grandchildren. She didn't mention all the church work, or the neighbors, family and friends I'm sure she cared for. The focus was on what she'd gotten paid for, or athletics, not the community and family-building activities we've participated in.

Living in a small town is hard. Everyone knows you, you never know if they're talking about you; the gossip can be vicious. Some of us flee those towns for the anonymity of the city, without realizing the price we pay. The emotional skills a small town can teach — tolerance, respect, resilience, the ability to work side by side with someone even when we disagree — are disappearing in our urban anonymity. Much of small town life happens through informal exchanges and self-reliance. Why did I go to my thirty-fifth high school reunion in St. Anthony, Idaho? Because as I get older I am more aware of the importance of small town culture, and also of the ways my own arrogance made life hard in a small town when I was younger.

The parallels between the domestication of animals, such as wolves to dogs, and the civilization of humans, is fascinating. In both cases the independence, autonomy and self-reliance of the wild version is striking. The wild version is able to survive independently. For the human version we see over the last two hundred years an increasing reliance on technology which paradoxically goes along with a decreased ability to act independently or to be self-sufficient. The movement from rural to urban for humans often includes a loss of self-reliance and an increasing dependence on financial exchanges and government, with a much more limited system of relationship/gift exchanges.

Hand sewing is one of my points of resistance to the monetary value system; gardening and canning are others. I make quilts by hand, first piecing, then putting the quilt back, batting and top together, basting and then hand quilting. I love not being tied to a machine when I sew, being able to take the work with me. We garden both in our yard and also in a community garden. In both cases what we produce is valued by the economic metric at far less than our time and effort would be worth. After visiting friends one weekend in 2017, they sent me home with a gift of tulsi (holy basil) seeds. The seeds were from their own plants, grown from seeds which had been received in a seed exchange. This felt like the right way to get sacred seeds — through gifts.

Hierarchy must be balanced with a commitment to the equality of all

Hierarchy can smooth functioning, but unless it is balanced by a commitment to the equal worth and value of all it will become problematic and eventually destructive. The concept of ownership is dependent on a belief in hierarchy, because one couldn't possibly own an equal being. To own and accumulate requires a judgment about lower worth of other beings, relegating them to the status of things.

Decolonizing Praxis

Looking at hierarchies, paying attention to any hints of non-hierarchy — sociocracy, other approaches.

Our chickens have a hierarchy, a pecking order. Rainer is the top chicken. This means she gets first dibs on all treats, and pushes the other chickens around. When we have treats, throwing them on the ground inside their fence, she will run to the first pile, then the second, and sometimes the third, checking to see which is best, and to make sure that is her portion. The other chickens will also run to whatever's thrown, but if Rainer comes toward whatever they're eating, they often move away. Jack, on the other hand, is at the bottom of the hierarchy. We have five chickens, a pair of Buff Orpingtons, a pair of Comets, and a single Orpington/Silver Lake cross. Jack is the single chicken, and I wonder sometimes if we did her a disservice. Is her different appearance part of why she's at the bottom, alone? Jack stays at the back when treats are thrown in, coming last, not pushing in, and backing off if one of the others threatens her.

Other animals have similar hierarchies, generally about status and access to resources. The hierarchies are more rigid when resources are scarce, and those at the top have first access. Over the millennia humans have evolved their own hierarchies to address the same question of access to scarce resources. Some 2,000 years ago, we are told that Jesus proposed a different solution to the challenge of distributing resources, and who you are obligated to share with. He answered "who is my neighbor?" in a very different way. He invited us to consider instead who we are, who we want to be, and what our best self would do. Instead of defining ourselves by symbolic goods, and our relative position in the status system, we define ourselves with reference to our best selves. Humans have been struggling with his invitation ever since. Is it realistic? Can we really live that way?

Challenging the Lies

These are the questions I'm walking with, feeling like I am only starting to scratch the surface of this work to listen and take faithful action. I must attend to when my underlying motivations are out of alignment with my deeper self and listen deeply for the actions I need to take. I am guided in all of this by the spiritual practices of the Quaker tradition, trusting in my experience that guidance comes and the next steps become clear.

Queries

What fundamental lies do you see in your life?
How are you grounding your life in eternal truths?

CHAPTER 13

Why the World Needs Quakerism

THE ROOM IN THE OXFORD QUAKER MEETING HOUSE is light-filled, with a group of twenty or so Friends sitting in a circle on a Friday evening in June. I'm grateful that my friend and elder Eleanor Godway is here, and thrilled Mary Penny, a professional colleague, has also chosen to come. We settle into worship after the tea and light refreshments, and I wait until I'm clear to share. We Quakers today are a pale shadow of who we are called to be. We are stewards of a powerful tradition, one that the world desperately needs. Three unique threads are embedded in our beliefs, structure and practices: (1) the invitation to walk together in ambiguity and paradox, (2) the knowledge that love is first, not belief, and (3) the ability to be together in a loose network of affiliations with a minimum of hierarchy.

When I reached out to British Friends in early 2015, looking for opportunities to gather with them in conjunction with a professional trip, Oxford Meeting was one of the two meetings that responded. John Mason and Anne Watson reached out as representatives of their Ministry and Counsel, and invited me to share as part of their regular "Friday with Friends" series. We put together a title and short description focusing on travel in the ministry for the advance publicity. The morning of the event I sat with what I was led to share, and the title came first. I played with different wordings: "The Amazing Gifts of the Quaker Tradition," "Strengths of the Quaker Tradition," "What Quakerism has to teach/offer the world." I settled on "Why the World Needs Quakerism, and Why We Need to be Better Quakers" as best capturing the gist of the threads I had been given as I sat in worship. Part of what I was led to lift up that evening is that each religious tradition at its founding holds the potential for a unique gestalt, a particular path to the Divine. Understanding the uniqueness of a tradition provides an important lens for considering multiple paths to the Divine, each with its own integrity.

I have carried the specific threads I was given for several years now, checking them with Friends from the different branches of Quakerism, and they continue to resonate. These threads are elements of the Quaker tradition; while each are present in other traditions, the Quaker combination provides a unique whole. The potential embodiment of each of these is embedded in the tradition, and has been present when we are working at our best. The three characteristics which I planned to talk about that morning are the following:

1. We have a process that allows us to walk together in uncertainty, ambiguity and paradox.

2. Love is first, not belief.

3. We have a relatively flat and localized structure, with the worshiping community at the center. We have maintained a global community with a minimum of hierarchy.

Two days later, on the same trip to England, I visited Ipswich Meeting for Sunday worship and a program following worship. As I listened in preparation Sunday morning, I realized I was being given the second part of the Friday evening message: *How* we can be better Quakers. This message was about the practices of Quakerism — we have a skills-based tradition, which relies on practical skills of tuning, discerning, listening and translating the Inner Christ, first at the individual level, and then at the corporate level. The fruits of these practices are transformed lives — lives lived from the Spirit.

The question of *why*, or even *if*, the world needs Quakerism has been discussed by Quaker scholars and theologians over the centuries. Early Friends such as Robert Barclay were clear Quakerism contained a unique restoration of the same living authority and power of God embodied in a religious tradition as early Christians experienced.[1] Over time perspectives shifted and Quakerism came to be viewed by some, including Rufus Jones, as a thread of the Christian mystical tradition.[2] Others such as John Punshon saw Quakerism as a

1 Robert Barclay, *Apology for the True Christian Divinity*, first published in 1678 (Farmington, ME: Quaker Heritage Press edition, 2002).

2 Rufus Jones, *A Call to What is Vital* (New York: The MacMillan Company, 1948); Rufus Jones, *The Faith and Practice of the Quakers* (Richmond, Indiana: Friends United Press, 1925).

strand of the Puritan movement.[3] Lewis Benson, in his 1961 essay "The Relation of Quakerism to Its Own History"[4] lifts up again the potential seen by Robert Barclay, of a tradition which can stand in the same power and authority as early Christian apostles. Howard Brinton's *Friends for 350 Years*[5] emphasized how in practice Quakerism seems to be balancing mysticism, activism, rationalism and evangelism, although he also saw the potential of embodying the same power and authority as early Christian apostles.

A Quaker Haiku

Wholehearted loving

Hear and move with the Spirit

The testimonies

If you ask those in many Quaker meetings today, a common answer about our uniqueness would be the Quaker testimonies, which we teach to our children with the acronym of SPICE and sometimes SPICES: Simplicity, Peace, Integrity, Community, Equality, and Stewardship.[6] We proudly proclaim our testimonies, particularly the peace testimony, to the world. They may be the closest thing we have to a creed. Some years ago I was on vacation, and chose to visit the closest meeting for worship on Sunday. I struck up a conversation with the clerk and asked about the life of the meeting. I had visited the meeting before, so the clerk felt free to share deeply. He was concerned about an application for membership the meeting had received from a veteran who had some cognitive disabilities due to military service. Some on the membership clearness committee and in the meeting were concerned this individual didn't fully subscribe to the

3 John Punshon, *Portrait in Grey: A Short History of the Quakers* (London: Quaker Home Service, 1984).

4 "The Relation of Quakerism to Its Own History," by Lewis Benson (1961), *Quaker Religious Thought*, Vol. 6, Article 4. Available at: http://digitalcommons.georgefox.edu/qrt/vol6/iss1/4 (Accessed 11/1/2017).

5 Howard Brinton and Margaret Hope Bacon, *Friends for 350 Years* (Pendle Hill: Pendle Hill Publications, 2002), chapter 10.

6 "The Origin of the Spices," by Paul Buckley (2012), delivered at South Central Yearly Meeting. Available online at https://www.concordfriendsmeeting.org/sites/all/files/documents/241.0496TheOriginOfTheSPICESbyPaulBuckley_bookfold.pdf (Accessed 11/1/2017).

peace testimony, and the individual might have cognitive difficulties understanding the peace testimony in situations of conflict. I was taken aback at the situation and shared my understanding: the testimonies grow out of a life lived in the Spirit, not the reverse. When we set a challenging goal, sometimes we can make it look right when the heart is completely wrong. Forcing ourselves to conform to the testimonies flips the order. The historical testimonies were the outward witness of an inward transformation by the Light of Christ, the Spirit, the Inward Teacher.

In Quakerism our words proclaim pride in our peace testimony, yet we have a dramatic history of divisions continuing in the present day, where even within our small communities we are unable to find a way to live into the truths of living with ambiguity, paradox, love and deep equality. People of color, business people, military members, political conservatives, and other groups have sometimes found themselves judged and excluded in Quaker settings. They are living witnesses to the difficulties Friends have had embodying the truths of our tradition. Since talking with Friends in Oxford in the summer of 2015, when I was first given the framing of these three elements of what the Quaker tradition carries, I have walked with each one. Each element has shown up in other places in my life, sending ripples which highlight the importance of these ideas. I have reflected on how each has been manifested historically and today, as well as what might be possible if Quakers could more fully embody these principles.

Uncertainty, Ambiguity and Paradox

We know how to walk together in uncertainty, ambiguity and paradox, in a world which loves certainty, even when it's wrong. Quakerism at its best, by disavowing creeds, challenges us to hear the Spirit in another, regardless of whether we agree with their beliefs, words or actions. Can we hear the Spirit in someone else's choices, even as they differ from our own? In addition to the emphasis on listening for the Spirit in the moment, Quaker business practice is structured in a way that provides a safe container for difference. Our business practice at its best seeks discernment on actions, not beliefs. A previous chapter, "Four Pillars of Meeting for Business," explored my understanding of Quaker business process, which has the potential to hold space for differences and for listening with deep respect and love. The truth sought through Quaker business process is the next step, the next action. In the focus on hearing the next step, we create a space which is able to hold paradox and ambiguity.

Quakerism has an emphasis on engaging authentically with others in our differences, similar to the Gospel order of early Christians. Some years ago, my home congregation was considering the question of whether to withhold donations to Friends United Meeting (FUM) because of strong ethical and moral objections to their personnel policy. I believe withholding funds to send a message to someone with whom one is in a relationship is manipulative, destructive to the relationship, and unlikely to lead to the changes we hope for. However, in a deeply memorable session for discernment, I sat next to a long-time Friend in his late eighties who believed deeply he needed to withhold his donation. I felt the Spirit moving in him as he spoke. Since then I have walked more intentionally in the ambiguous space of disagreeing with the FUM policy and being clear to support FUM financially, while also knowing other Quakers may be led to withhold funds.

One of the places Quakers today are directly challenged to walk in ambiguity and paradox is around the question of Christianity. There are Quakers who are deeply Christian and others who see themselves as not Christian at all. Walking together across these varied beliefs requires an ability to hold paradox and ambiguity together. In April 2014, I was in a Friends World Committee for Consultation Section of the Americas workshop on cross-cultural communication in High Point, North Carolina. We were invited to think about the range of cultures in our own meetings. The conversation soon turned to Friends who felt their Christianity was being suppressed because others in their meeting were hurt by Christian language. After listening for some time, Carlos Moran,[7] a Latin American friend rose and spoke in translation. He started by saying he heard what people were saying, and he thought he understood. But he didn't understand, because his relationship with Jesus had nothing to do with the relationship to Jesus of the people around him — their relationship with Jesus was up to them. His message fundamentally changed the tenor

---

7 This anecdote is shared with the permission of Carlos Moran.

in the room, as he encouraged Friends to more faithfully walk with what they're given, while loving others in the community who see things differently.

In the fall of 2015 my husband and I were visiting close friends in Cambridge, Massachusetts. Their Department of Public Works (DPW) composts residential food waste if residents bring it to the DPW disposal site. My friends Jennifer and Ed are very diligent in composting and taking food waste to the DPW on a weekly basis. Their DPW also has an area set aside for free-cycling, where individuals can leave gently used books and household goods for others to take. Jennifer, as a high school English teacher, enjoys going through the books on a regular basis. This particular visit Jennifer offered to loan me one of her recent DPW acquisitions, a review copy of *Nonsense: The Power of Not-Knowing*, by Jamie Holmes. I accepted the synchronicity and took the book home. *Nonsense* focuses on the challenges uncertainty causes, and particularly on the ways in which ambiguity creates anxiety and affects decision making. I devoured the book, as it spoke so directly to the importance of building the skills of holding uncertainty and ambiguity. The following spring, Alder Keleman, an amazing PhD student I had the honor of working with, recommended another book on ambiguity and uncertainty, Annie Tsing's *The Mushroom at the End of the World*. Tsing uses the example of the matsutake mushroom economy to illuminate the growing uncertainty in today's global economy. The matsutake grows in groves of pine and, much more seldom, oak trees of a particular maturity and density. Such groves have disappeared in Japan, but conditions for matsutake growth are prime in the second growth forests of the Pacific Northwest. Matsutake cultivation, given the complex partnership with trees, doesn't fit within the western agricultural paradigm of controlled monoculture. The collection, processing, marketing and distribution system which has developed around matsutake is resoundingly in the informal economy, where individuals collect mushrooms and independent agents consolidate. As independent contractors, the individuals cannot count on regular paychecks, health benefits or retirement plans, and the individual agents speak of the freedom they feel. There is uncertainty about the hunt for matsutake, and with uncertainty comes an economic uncertainty. The matsutake economy is emblematic of the growing global economic uncertainty, where individuals are struggling to support themselves and to live. *Nonsense* suggests that we each have a base level of tolerance for ambiguity, and outside our comfort zone we tend to make much more conservative decisions. In such a climate, a greater ability to function with uncertainty would be very beneficial. Holmes notes in *Nonsense* that we can work to enlarge our comfort zone, which then expands the options we will consider for decisions. Paul Levy's *Dispelling Wetigo*[8] compares two-point and four-point logic. Two-point logic has two options, (1) yes or (2) no. Four-point logic has (1) yes, (2) no, (3) yes and no, and (4) neither yes nor no. Being able to accept options three and four allows us to break out of dualistic thinking and to consider more complex truths. Similarly, by focusing on listening deeply to each other and the Spirit, while seeking to avoid two-point logic creedal tests, there is potential for transformation which is sorely needed in times of personal, community, national and global uncertainty and change.

Love Is First, Not Belief

The second core element of Quakerism focuses on loving others. In George Fox's journal where he speaks of his experience of coming through the ocean of darkness, he describes coming into an ocean of light and love.[9] We sometimes forget the "love" part of the quotation. We each have a hunger to be loved, and we have an image of the love we want — generally unending and nonjudgmental. *Long Life Honey in the Heart*, by Martin Prechtel, tells his story of participating fully in the ritual life of Guatemalan villagers in the 1970s. The book is oriented around the initiation ritual, whereby youth are started on their path to being adult, which means being fully human. One is brought to her first initiation when she starts showing interest in romantic relationships, an indication she is becoming aware of the hollow in her heart, and seeking to fill it. Youths who are not initiated will try to fill the hollow with other people, never realizing the hollow is for God.

8 Paul Levy, *Dispelling Wetigo: Breaking the Curse of Evil* (Berkeley, CA: North Atlantic Books, 2013), pp. 40–44.

9 George Fox, *Journal*, edited by John L. Nickalls (Philadephia: Religious Society of Friends, 1997), p. 19.

In each of our hearts there is a yearning for unconditional love and acceptance. We know in our bones and deep in our hearts what it feels like. And yet when we turn to people for this kind of love, be it parents, friends, lovers or our children, we are doomed to disappointment. In our humanness we will fail each other; we're not there when needed, or we judge others.

While the unconditional love we yearn for can only come from God, religious communities, families and other human relationships are important laboratories for practicing. It is in our personal relationships we practice acting from a place of unconditional love. Religious communities can create a place where we are more able to trust.

It is much easier to share the love in our bones with strangers. These people will come into our lives and leave them without there being a possibility of our coming to expect too much of them. And as long as we can give without expectation, we can move with Divine peace. With our friends and loved ones we have expectations — of how they will act, of what they will do for us, and of what their actions mean. The expectations can intervene between the Divine center and our actions. I place my own judgments of others between the Divine in me and the Divine in others, and this is most apparent in my closest relationships. Seeing the ways my thoughts and behaviors are out of alignment with my deeply held beliefs requires regular practice. Remembering and living from a centered place of love can take a lifetime of transformation. Changing the thoughts and behaviors is a lifetime journey which can be supported by a religious community.

When Isaac Penington tried to capture the everyday joy of early Friends, he said "Our life is love and peace and tenderness."[10] I hear descriptions of Quaker youth retreats and some adult retreats being able to capture the life of love and peace and tenderness Penington spoke of. Such retreats can be a valuable learning laboratory, particularly when participants learn from the intentionality of the guidelines and container around the retreat. When John Woolman wrestled with questions of whether he had a clear leading to travel in the ministry visiting with the Indians in the Pennsylvania wilderness, part of his justification for the authenticity of the leading was "Love was the

10 Isaac Penington, *Letters*, edited by John Barclay, 1828, p. 139; 3rd 3dn, 1844, p. 138 (Letter LII, to Friends in Amersham, dated Aylesbury, 4 iii [May] 1667).

first motion."[11] His intention was not conversion, or the need to preach, but rather a desire to reach out with love. When I listen for my own intentions and motives, similar to Woolman, I often find it difficult to be certain as I wade through the twisted motivations and logic of my own heart. It always feels like a gift filled with grace when I come to a place of knowing love is the first motion.

While the rhetoric in Quakerism is about loving each other, sometimes the reality is not. Mike Huber, pastor of West Hills Friends Church in Portland, Oregon, gave a sermon in March 2017 on authority and listening in love, where he reminded the congregation (and all who listen) of the importance of putting love first in our interactions with each other, while noting patterns of behavior within his meeting where love might not be coming first.[12] I have noted through the years times when my Mormon siblings demonstrate in their daily lives the practice of the non-judgmental love Quakers aspire to. One of the more profound examples was when a childless sister and her husband took in a teenage boy who was accused of sexual assaulting a relative. He was no longer able to live with his family, and when a church leader asked my sister and brother-in-law to help, they did. The boy lived with them for some months. I have shared the story with a number of Quakers, none of whom have thought they would be willing to do the same.

A Very Limited Hierarchy

The third element of this Quaker gestalt is an organizational structure with a limited hierarchy. Quakerism has a relatively flat and localized structure, with the worshiping community at the center. Quaker monthly meetings are the primary authority, particularly among liberal yearly meetings. Some yearly meetings do have a hierarchy, where the yearly meeting is understood to have authority over the monthly meetings. This variation and ambiguity about hierarchy is important in reminding Quakers how at our best we are all

11 John Woolman, *Journal and Major Essays of John Woolman*, edited by Phillips P. Moulton (Richmond, IN: Friends United Press, 1989), p. 121–22.

12 "On Authority and Listening in Love" by Mike Huber, accessed June 30, 2017. https://soundcloud.com/westhillsfriends/on-authority-and-listening-in-love-by-mike-huber

listening for the same Spirit. It is also unique in maintaining a diffusion of power and authority. While hierarchical structures may be able to smooth functioning, the nature of the structure values people at different places (higher and lower) in the hierarchy differently. This differential valuing across a hierarchy has historically led to oppression and the justification of rewards and benefits for those at the top, generally drawn from mandated or expected sacrifices of those below them. The differential valuing based on position is the foundation of oppression. Quakerism's limited hierarchy emphasizes the intrinsic worth and equality of all human beings, and the knowledge of worth is integrated into the structure. Complex societal and organizational hierarchies can violate the truth of the intrinsic worth and equality of all. John MacMurray, a Scottish Quaker philosopher, writes in *The Clue to History* of the importance of distinguishing between personal equality and functional equality. While knowledge or expertise may place someone in a position of functional power, the functional inequality does not mean someone is of less worth as a human being. Care for the personal equality of all is embedded in the Quaker structure. There are downsides to the lack of hierarchy, particularly when there are questions of poor functioning. If there is no external authority, who is able to challenge a community which is out of alignment, particularly when the community does not see itself as out of alignment with Truth?

Conclusions

None of these three elements are unique to Quakerism. They provide a different, perhaps more pragmatic, perspective on what Quakerism has to contribute. I cannot accept the traditional exceptionalism of the power and authority of early Christians others have spoken to, perhaps because of my experience of the same claims within Mormonism. Paul Levy's four-point logic allows me to hold the potential in Quakerism and Mormonism (and all other religious traditions), that when believers are faithfully living in the vital stream of their origins, they can carry the power and authority of the Divine. The exceptionalism I embrace is a constellation of structure, practice and belief that can provide a different way of walking in the world, embodying the living and vital Spirit in a uniquely Quaker way. To build on the metaphor of grafting from "On Being Grafted into the Root," Quakerism is a unique and valued rootstock, and Quakers need to be grafted in to live into the fruitfulness of the Quaker tree. The alignment, and grafting in, is a lifelong journey, inviting us to ripen into bearing the fruits of the potential of the Quaker tradition. We live in a world deeply in need of the truths Quakerism can attest to when we are fully embracing this vital and living tradition.

Many Quakers today have been grafted in to the Quaker tree from another religious tradition. And even if someone has always been part of the Quaker tradition, we all need to attend to the grafting Robert Barclay spoke of, "To forsake unrighteousness and be turned to righteousness, and, in the inwardness of the mind, to be cut out of the wild olive tree of our own first fallen nature and ingrafted into Christ by his Word and Spirit in the heart."[13] We need to be willing to be fully grafted in to whatever tradition we are drawn to. We need to bear the fruits of our tradition. Within Quakerism, the challenge of coming in to this tradition with no catechism or structured teaching program to help us come to know the unique fruit, sometimes makes it difficult to accept the responsibility to be the tree and to bear the fruit.

Quakerism is rooted in personal transformation. Hearing the Spirit requires that we then take action based on what we hear with the inward ear, and that we change our lives to be ever more responsive to the promptings. Our eternal work is to transform ourselves, to move from being convinced of the reality of the Living Christ in our hearts to converting our lives to be centered around the Living Presence. We are called to come into the Presence. And then we are called to move out into the world, holding ourselves in the Living Stream, moving in tune with the Divine. This is how Quakers have always been transformed, and the world around them.

Grafting in to the Quaker tradition roots us in the Judeo-Christian path in a powerful way. Early Quakers would have known of Jesus's use of the word "Friends" — Friends today are less aware. We are called to be Friends, as Jesus used the term when he said to his disciples, "I will no longer call you servants, because the servant doesn't understand the Master's purpose. I will call you Friends, because

13 Barclay, loc.cit.

everything I have learned from my Father I have shared with you."[14] Growing in to the xylem and phloem of the Divine Source gives us a direct connection.

We are called to be Friends, to hold the truths of our traditions together in one tree. The truths of the Hebrew prophets who knew God's laws are woven into the fabric of the Universe — how our society looks and whether it is oppressive grows out of whether we are in right relationship with the Divine Source. We are called to bring those truths together with the truths that Jesus brought — God's purpose is to build the kingdom of heaven on earth, and the kingdom is both within and without. We are called to hold together the truths George Fox and the early Quakers knew, as they had the kingdom of heaven open to them. We are called to sit with these truths, to grow into the rootstock of these truths, to hear the vision of the kingdom for our time. We are called to open the kingdom. This is the fruit of the Quaker tree.

Queries

What are your experiences of the unique threads of Quakerism?

In your daily life, how do you manifest the principle that love, not belief, comes first?

How comfortable are you with ambiguity and paradox? How does your meeting hold ambiguity and paradox as a community?

Who can assess alignment with Truth of another?

How do we hold each other accountable to the authority and power of the Spirit?

14 John 15:15.

Epilogue

THE ESSAYS HEREIN are offered as a modern example of a paradigmatic spiritual journey. Each of us has an open invitation from the Divine to engage in a rich and rewarding life of the Spirit. They are snapshots from an ongoing journey. As I have brought these pieces together I have been challenged by an awareness of the hubris of sharing my own experience as an example. Reworking earlier essays describing my own spiritual practices had me struggling with the way putting ideas into words on paper in print gives them solidity. I rediscovered once again the importance of expanding my morning time during times of high pressure and anxiety. My spiritual practices these days are fluid, with morning time listening outside in my pavilion and often a sense of inadequacy and internal questions of whether I am actually living what I am writing about in these pages. This book chronicles both my lived experiences and my aspirations.

I know from my own experience that deep listening can lead to amazing openings into love and truth. I hunger for a world where we are encouraged to take our spiritual lives seriously, while also taking scriptural traditions seriously but not literally / factually. I believe deeply in the potential of the Quaker tradition to transform lives and the world. I believe Quakerism has a unique combination of teachings that can help humans live into a more just, loving, and healthy world. The Quaker gestalt — the belief that love is first, the practice of deep listening, and the adherence to a limited hierarchy — together embody a profound respect for the sacred in each of us. Quakerism does this while also holding the loving awareness that we are often not our best selves, and that listening deeply to ourselves and others can help to call the sacred forth.

Glossary

AFSC: American Friends Service Committee

clerk: The leader of communities and meetings in Quaker communities and organizations. "The clerk of a meeting performs an administrative function in a way that also provides spiritual leadership."[1]

corporate discernment: Quakers use the term "corporate" to refer to the *corpus*, the entire body, of the community. Corporate discernment is thus the process by which the community makes decisions as a body.

experiments with Light: A reflective process developed by Rex Ambler, and described in *Light to Live By*,[2] which draws extensively on the reflective process used by early Quakers. The process involves asking the Light for guidance on particular issues, and waiting to see what the Light reveals.

Faith and Practice **(F&P):** While Quakers traditionally do not have creeds, Yearly Meetings generally do adopt books of discipline, often called books of *Faith and Practice*. The process for developing these books can take years, as the Faith and Practice Committee prepares text, and then submits it for discernment to the yearly meeting. These books generally describe the practices and procedures used in the yearly meeting. They may include quotations from Quaker literature and contain "advices" and "queries." (Guidance and questions to help Friends examine themselves and their lives as they strive to live more fully in the Light).[3]

FCNL: Friends Committee on National Legislation

FGC: Friends General Conference

1 This definition taken from http://www.quakerinfo.org/resources/glossary

2 Rex Ambler, *Light to Live By* (Quaker Books, March 2002). Additional guidance on the process is provided at http://www.experiment-with-light.org.uk/medits.htm

3 Adapted from http://www.quakerinfo.org/quakerism/faithandpractice

FUM: Friends United Meeting
FWCC: Friends World Committee for Consultation

meeting for business: Short for meeting for worship for the conduct of business, where Friends gather to conduct business of the community.

meeting for worship: "This event is the period in which the Friends community gathers to take part in a religious observance. It parallels the Catholic mass or Protestant church service. In different branches of Friends, meeting for worship takes different forms. . . . In addition to regularly scheduled (generally weekly) meetings for worship, many Friends may hold worship together at the beginning and end of committee meetings, at the beginning of class in a Friends school, and on other occasions, sometimes spontaneously."[4]

monthly, quarterly and yearly meeting: Quaker congregations are organized into a nested community, from local congregations that meet to conduct business on a monthly schedule (monthly meetings), to regional meetings that conduct business quarterly (quarterly meetings), and larger regional meetings that conduct business annually (yearly meetings).

New England Yearly Meeting (NEYM): Vermont, New Hampshire, Maine, Massachusetts, Rhode Island, Connecticut.

New York Yearly Meeting (NYYM): New York, New Jersey, Connecticut.

queries: Formal questions that are designed to encourage deeper reflection. Quakers use queries as both individual and group tools for centering and reflection. Some meetings will start a meeting for business or meeting for worship by reading a query.

Southern Appalachian Yearly Meeting and Association (SAYMA): A combination of meetings in West Virginia, Kentucky, Tennessee, Georgia, North Carolina, Alabama, South Carolina, and Mississippi.

waiting worship: A style of worship where worshipers sit together, waiting on the Spirit. The Spirit may lead one of those present into vocal ministry, or the worship may be completely silent.

---

4 Quoted in http://www.quakerinfo.org/resources/glossary

worship & ministry (W&M); ministry & counsel (M&C): While names vary by meeting, these committees are responsible for holding and nurturing the quality of ministry in a Quaker meeting.[5]

worship sharing: A structured format used for small group sharing that includes an opening period of centering worship, a period when individuals are invited to share — generally in response to a specific query — and then closing in worship. Worship sharing involves sharing deeply and personally, without responding to what others share. Guidelines encourage individuals to share once and then wait until all others present have shared (or chosen to pass) before sharing again.

Quaker terms and phrases available online:

From the Earlham School of Religion:

http://www.quakerinfo.org/resources/glossary

Philadelphia Yearly Meeting has compiled a style manual for Quaker publications and terms, available online at:

http://www.pym.org/publications/pym-pamphlets/ quaker-manual-of-style-and-glossary/

Two glossaries of Quaker terms developed by meetings are available here:

http://downingtownfriendsmeeting.org/glossary.htm
http://www.ogmm.org/quaker-glossary/

Mormon Terminology and Acronyms:

family home evening: A weekly family gathering generally with a lesson, activity and refreshments.

general authorities: The highest levels of religious leaders within the world-wide church.

bishop: Leader of a local congregation.

Church of Jesus Christ of Latter Day Saints (LDS): Full name of the Mormon Church.

Brigham Young University (BYU): Private university owned and run by the Mormon Church.

---

5 More information can be found at https://newym.org/ministry-counsel

Permissions

Chapter 1: *Soul Time*

Adapted from a *Friends Journal* article titled "A Place for Soul Time," August 2001. Used by permission of *Friends Journal*.

Chapter 6: *Our Hope for a New Life*

Adapted from a *Quaker Life* article titled "Our Hope for a New Life," May–June 2008. Used by permission of *Quaker Life*.

Chapter 7: *On Being Grafted Into the Root*

Adapted from a Beacon Hill Friends House pamphlet titled "On Being Grafted Into the Root," Spring 2008. Used by permission of Beacon Hill Friends House.

Chapter 8: *Engaging with a Monthly Meeting about Ministry*

Adapted from a *Friends Journal* article titled "Engaging with a Monthly Meeting about Ministry," September 2008, by Debbie Humphries & Diane Randall. Used by permission of *Friends Journal*.

Chapter 9: *Four Pillars of Meeting for Business*

Adapted from a *Friends Journal* article titled "Four Pillars of Meeting for Business," September 2009. Used by permission of *Friends Journal*.

Chapter 11: *Exploring the Unwritten Rules of Waiting Worship*

Adapted from a *Friends Journal* article titled "Exploring the Unwritten Rules of Meeting for Worship," August 2014. Used by permission of *Friends Journal*.

Acknowledgements

THIS BOOK WOULD NOT BE POSSIBLE without the support and encouragement of so many friends and family. I am very grateful to my husband, John, and our sons, Rainer and CJ, for their accompaniment on my spiritual journey. They met me at the end of the trail, cuddled with me in the mornings, and have been stalwart in their patience, love and encouragement.

I thank the Friends who have served on my support committee from Hartford Monthly Meeting (Francis Helfrick, Eleanor Godway, Roz Spier, Martin Wheeler, John Stamm, David Holdt, Daphne Bye, Diane Weinholtz, Bonniejean Dibelius, and Cruger Philips). The friends who have walked with me both metaphorically and literally through the years have been important companions as I have read and reflected on the ideas shared here. Jennifer Hogue, Daphne Bye, and Miela Gruber, I can't thank you enough. I am grateful to the family and friends who read versions of these essays over the last seventeen years, for their careful and thoughtful feedback. Marty Grundy, Hinckley Jones-Sanpei, Linda Quinton Burr, Rachel Pia, Lloyd Lee Wilson, and Anna Moberly all read the most recent versions of the manuscript and provided feedback on the full manuscript. Any shortcomings herein are mine, and are fewer for their efforts.

About the Author

D EBBIE HUMPHRIES GREW UP MORMON and came to Quakerism in the early 1990s. Since then she has been a member of meetings in New York, West Virginia and Connecticut, serving on numerous committees of Hartford Monthly Meeting and New England Yearly Meeting. Debbie has travelled in the ministry among Quakers since 2004 under the care of Hartford Monthly Meeting, carrying a concern for the spiritual health and vitality of the Religious Society of Friends. Debbie teaches at the Yale School of Public Health and conducts research on public health nutrition, nutrition and infectious disease, and community health, both within the United States and internationally.

CPSIA information can be obtained
at www.ICGtesting.com
Printed in the USA
FFOW04n0136241217
44169417-43553FF